The Weight of Sand

EDITH BLAIS

Translated by KATIA GRUBISIC

The Weight of Sand

My 450 Days Held Hostage in the Sahara

GREYSTONE BOOKS

Vancouver/Berkeley

First published in English by Greystone Books in 2021
Originally published in French as *Le Sablier*, copyright © 2021 by Éditions
de l'Homme, a division of Groupe Sogides, Inc., Montreal, Quebec, Canada
English translation copyright © 2021 by Katia Grubisic
Illustrations copyright © 2021 by Edith Blais

21 22 23 24 25   5 4 3 2 1

Greystone Books Ltd.
greystonebooks.com

Cataloguing data available from Library and Archives Canada
ISBN 978-1-77164-909-4 (cloth)
ISBN 978-1-77164-910-0 (epub)

Original editing by Ann Châteauvert
Editing for English edition by Paula Ayer
Poetry editing for English edition by Broc Rossell
Proofreading by Jennifer Stewart

Jacket and text design by Jessica Sullivan
Jacket photograph by Krystel V. Morin
Photograph on page 155 courtesy of the family of Edith Blais
Printed in Canada on FSC® certified paper at Friesens. The FSC® label
means that materials used for the product have been responsibly sourced.

Greystone Books gratefully acknowledges the Musqueam, Squamish,
and Tsleil-Waututh peoples on whose land our office is located.

Greystone Books thanks the Canada Council for the Arts, the British Columbia
Arts Council, the Province of British Columbia through the Book Publishing Tax
Credit, and the Government of Canada for supporting our publishing activities.

To my Lady Light, Sophie Pétronin, and to my heavenly star, Sister Gloria Cecilia Narvaez. Your shining strength and courage rekindled my spirit. Thank you for having sown the seed which, thanks to your endless encouragements beneath that white tent, blossomed into The Weight of Sand. *May my love accompany you and yours. I will hold you forever in my heart and in my thoughts.*

Contents

I Am Myself

I walked, walked to find my path
Through the woods and in the looming mist.
Beneath the mystery above the stars,
Through concrete cities' endless drift.

I walked, walked and never looked back.
I burned my feet on the desert sand,
Swayed my body in the ocean's swell and slack.
I walked, walked to find my land ...

I looked for myself everywhere,
Went after the wind as it wove in the streets
And through the dunes' deep nowhere
To the far horizons I would meet.

From the wise world, riddles fell
And set me on a path with new meaning.
Wherever I looked, I found myself:
I am here, I am there, I am me in the wind.

PART I

Europe–Togo

[1]

Crossroads

WHEN I WAS twenty-nine years old, I went on a trip.

"I'm going away for the summer," I told my family and friends. "I'm going to pick cherries in the Okanagan. I'll be back in Quebec in the fall."

They looked at me wryly; they doubted I'd really be back by fall. I couldn't blame them. I had said the same thing to them when I was eighteen and only returned a year and a half later. I tried to reassure them: I'd already bought a non-refundable return ticket for September.

So I set off for the summer. I met amazing people. But my friends and my family obviously knew me better than I thought, since I didn't come home by fall. Once I'd had a taste of adventure, I was hooked: the freedom spoke to my soul. Traveling was intoxicating, and I didn't want it to stop—I wasn't full yet. I wanted to discover what was happening elsewhere in the world, in other cultures. Who would I be blessed enough to meet? What unique landscapes might I behold? On what soil might I tread? How would traveling change the way I thought about life, about the world?

I was free—the wind in my hair, my tent in my pack, my thumb stuck out. I was about to venture out on the mythical Route 101 along the Pacific coast of the United States toward California.

In the fall of 2014, I met a man in Northern California through a mutual friend. He was from Togo, where he'd been working on a permaculture project, based on the principles of agroforestry. He wanted to develop a self-sufficient farm, producing food and renewable energy, and he dreamed of founding a local ecological center that would promote the exchange of knowledge between travelers and villagers in the Kpalimé region. He also hoped to reforest a seventy-acre plot with native fruit trees. The project should be underway within a few years, he thought. When the time came, he would even take in travelers who wanted to give him a hand. He'd mentioned the idea to the perfect person: I could already imagine myself working on his promised, promising land. I wanted to discover African culture, to which I'd been drawn since I was young, and I wanted to help my friend fulfill his dream of a place where it was possible to live simply and in tune with nature.

I had always believed that a simpler existence would make me see life in a different light, and I wanted to take a break from a culture that seemed materialistic to me. I wanted to share with others, to get closer to the earth, to eat with my hands, to walk barefoot, to feed on the elements. To live without chairs, without a table, a sofa, without a TV and a bed, no roof, no door, no shower. Though I expected I would miss showers.

Sure, my vision was a touch romantic, but that's just the way I am: I've always been carried along by dreams, and nourished by reality. I also wanted to spend time with my Togolese friend—I thought the world of him—and to help make his dream come true. I had even just finished a horticulture course that spring. I didn't have much experience, but I wanted to learn, and to keep learning. I'd been craving a connection to the earth, to life, to the planet and its secrets, its mysteries and its beauty. I wanted to stir up the endurance and the resourcefulness that I knew lay dormant within me. I wanted to breathe, to take in life far away from pollution, from comfort, and from people who are always in a rush.

With a light heart, I left the friends with whom I had traveled to California, and went on alone. Mexico, Guatemala, El Salvador, Honduras, Nicaragua, Costa Rica, Panama... I had lots of adventures, and I met unforgettable people. I danced with incredible folk musicians. I practiced acro-yoga on the beach in Mexico where a bunch of us had gathered at sunset. I went down to Guatemala with two Spaniards, a Swiss guy, and a Japanese. We thought of ourselves as a bohemian caravan.

I saw awe-inspiring nature, the world revealed sumptuously before my amazed eyes. I slept on beaches, under the glimmer of the stars, and woke up in the morning with dew clinging to my sleeping bag, my face uncovered. I loved it! There is nothing more soothing than falling asleep to the sound of waves as they settle gently on the sand. I also slept in slightly more unusual places—orchards, volcanoes, under trucks, on boats, under bridges...

One night, I'd planned to sleep on the beach in Santa Barbara. I'd spotted a police cruiser, and hid under a boat. But the cop car turned in my direction and the headlights caught me. The police kindly explained that I had to go to sleep with the homeless people, on the main street, under a streetlight. I would be safer there; and, above all, the law was the law. I couldn't believe it. What could be safer than my hiding place under the boat? But the police said they would kick me off the beach again if I came back to sleep here: it was illegal. So I hauled my backpack along and curled up on the cold concrete, trying to hide in my sleeping bag so that no one would notice I was a young woman alone. I understood then why people who live on the street sleep on cardboard boxes: the cold concrete is freezing, and the cardboard provides some insulation. I didn't sleep a wink that night. I was worried, listening in on the conversations my new roommates were having with their ghosts. I would have preferred the lapping of the waves, but things don't always work out the way you want.

For several years, I traveled, and every summer, I came back to Canada to work out west. Then, in July 2016, I met Luca, in the Rockies. It was one of those encounters that changes your life.

I needed money after traveling abroad, and that spring I found myself in the small town of Jasper, in Alberta. I found work in a hotel kitchen, and in a restaurant I liked because the chef shared my values. He cooked from the heart, with local, organic products, and the dishes he created were inspiring, unusual, and beautiful.

As spring turned to summer, I quit both jobs: I was leaving for British Columbia to go cherry picking in the Okanagan. My boss at the hotel wished me a safe trip, but the chef asked me to stay. He caught me off guard: I liked him and I didn't want to leave him in the lurch. I would think about it, I replied. But I had nowhere to live, since I'd been staying in an apartment provided for hotel employees.

I had fallen in love with Jasper and its surroundings, so accepting the chef's proposal was a no-brainer. Jasper is the kind of place where there's only one traffic light, and there are elk constantly wandering through the streets, as if here, animals and humans lived together in harmony. The soul of Jasper is authentic, and the region is backdropped by crystal-clear rivers, turquoise lakes, and mountains that brush the sky. The air was good, fresh and pure. After work, I only had to walk five minutes to find myself in the heart of an astounding wilderness.

A few days later, a nice lady offered to let me pitch my tent on her property while I was looking for a place to stay. In exchange, I offered to help her with her work. Every problem has a solution, but sometimes you have to use your imagination.

The next day, I came across a want ad: a small organic café was looking for a barista. And they offered accommodation! It was perfect. Everything was falling into place.

When you meet someone who is going to change your life, the moment seems electric, illuminated, charged with a special significance. That's what happened the day I met a handsome young man with an exotic—and to be honest, kind of charming—accent, standing behind the counter at the café. My memory of meeting Luca will remain etched in my mind forever.

We worked together at the little café, and we were neighbors: I lived in number 108 and he lived in 110. We were always knocking on each other's door. A strong, unique friendship grew between us.

Jasper isn't very big; you can walk across the whole town in under an hour. Whenever we went somewhere together, I always told Luca that I wanted to walk, while he preferred to ride his bike. Obviously I always ended up being convinced: he was that cute. So I would sit on the handlebars while Luca wheeled me around Jasper. In time, we became experts at our balancing act. One night, we were riding in the dark, beneath the northern lights. They were beautiful, waltzing and waving above us and the little bicycle that ferried us home.

Luca and I saw the northern lights another time, too. We'd asked our boss, who by then had become a good friend, to lend us his car. Luca had to fly to Edmonton to return home to Italy, while I was going to be working in Jasper for a few more months. Before we left, our boss mentioned that twice the accelerator had gotten stuck, and that the car smelled like gas. If by chance the pedal got stuck, all we had to do was shift into neutral. And if the smell of gas bothered us, we could just roll down the windows, even though it was still winter. The car made a racket, our friend added, shrieking like something monstrous. I found the warnings alarming, but Luca wasn't worried.

"Come on, Edith, it'll be fine! The pedal won't get stuck. And if it does, we know what to do."

"Luca, I don't want us to drive this car, it's going to croak on us. I'm not even sure it should legally be on the road."

We left for Edmonton, a four-hour drive from Jasper, Luca driving the deathtrap and me on the passenger side, breathing cold air through a gap in the window we'd cracked open. I affectionately christened the car the Red Dragon.

That night, the Alberta sky lit up for Luca, bidding him farewell. The brightly colored aurora borealis unfurled over the Red Dragon. The scene was so awesome that we stopped several times by the side of the road to get a better look at the ribbons winding their way through the sky. The northern lights filled us with wonder through the whole ride. Life had given us quite a show.

We said goodbye at the airport early in the morning, but it wasn't the last time I would see Luca, nor the last time we would be apart. Our relationship was both simple and complex, sometimes romantic and sometimes platonic. When we were separated by a continent or an ocean, we were good friends, but when we found each other again, the romance was rekindled, usually right where we had left off. Sometimes, in the course of things, the handsome Luca would declare his love to another girl—like the first time I joined him in Italy. So then we remained good friends, as we had always been.

Luca and I had traveled together several times before we started our journey across Africa. In 2016, we had gone to visit a cousin of his on Vancouver Island. In 2017, Luca introduced me to his family in Italy. In 2016 and 2017, we went to California, where he met my Togolese friend—who that year was finally ready to tackle his big project. Luca and I wanted to be part of it. The two of them talked about the possibility of making the trip to Togo from Italy by car. What a great idea, and what an incredible adventure! A bit risky, perhaps. But we would be careful.

My uncle had been living in Africa for several years, working in development with his wife, and I knew he would give us good advice. And our Togolese friend knew the countries well. I was confident, and enthusiastic.

My guardian angel was utterly exhausted.

Little Nomad

SEPTEMBER 12, 2019
269th day in captivity

Little nomad, you bear my name.
We share a life, our goals and dreams.
You glide with me through the cold rain
And our reflection glistens in the street.

You're on the move, day and night,
And in my dreams you find new roads.
You live to love and you love life—
The earth's every detour is yours to roam.

My little nomad, the wind's at your feet
And you like that, you're at ease.
It swaddles you in all its secrets,
Your fingers in the trailing breeze...

You ask the forbidden to stay,
Map a life to match your steps.
You discover the world, dancing in a way
That shows your spirit is boundless.

Little nomad, your path is untraced.
Your footprints, while I remained,
Were lost in the sand, erased—
You forgot my face and lost my name.

11

[2]

Itinerary

THE JOURNEY TO AFRICA was about to begin. It was November 19, 2018, and we were getting ready to celebrate a birthday: Luca and his twin sister were turning thirty. There would be a big party at the family home in northern Italy—a memorable celebration—and the next day we would leave for Genoa, where Luca's cousin lived.

Our itinerary was set: first Italy, then France, where Luca would visit his younger sister in Toulouse, then Spain, where we had friends. Our last European destination was Tarifa, at the southern tip of Spain. From there we could already see Africa—the Moroccan coast, since the Strait of Gibraltar is only about eight miles at its narrowest point. And from Tarifa, we would take the ferry to Tangier.

Our Togolese friend had given us the contact information of a friend of his, a German who traveled regularly between Morocco and Ghana to go see his Ghanaian wife and their children. Morocco, Mauritania, the southern tip of Mali, Burkina Faso, and finally Ghana: his itinerary boosted our confidence. The only difference between his trip and ours was that we would go from Burkina Faso straight to Togo, without stopping in Ghana, because the land border was tightly controlled and permits were expensive. My uncle had also been kind enough to share information and advice. He was used to Africa, and to traveling. He'd suggested the same route, with just a few differences. As for equipment, our car contained, among other things, a GPS installed especially for our trip, three spare tires, a jerry can of gas, plenty of water, and everything we needed to fix the car if it broke down. We were ready to go! Or so we hoped.

We drove through Europe without any pitfalls. The trip was such a joy. In the Pyrenees, Luca showed me places he had seen when he had cycled through with a friend a few years earlier. They'd left Padua by train and traveled down to Genoa, where they set out on two wheels. They had biked through Nice, Montpellier, Toulouse, the Pyrenees, Zaragoza, Barcelona, Valencia, Granada, Córdoba, and Seville. Luca wasn't one to fear adventure; he didn't fear anything. I was glad to be traveling with him.

When we got to Andalusia, the old, labyrinthine White Towns were alive with warmth and jubilation. I heartily recommend the streets of Andalusia to romantics and dreamers. As we strolled along, we came across Romani sitting on low walls strumming their guitars, couples in love, and artisans in front of their enchanting stalls. The sun gleamed bright against the windows.

On our way across Andalusia, I came across a scorpion-woman. Night draped slowly down while we were having a drink on a small terrace. Our conversation was suddenly interrupted by the sounds of castanets, clapping, and cries. In the distance, a small crowd had gathered around a flamenco dancer and her musicians. Intrigued, I approached, and climbed up on a stool. Luca helped me keep my balance. That's when I saw her: the dancer was drubbing the ground with her feet and clapping her hands, her arms moving like claws, as if she were about to pounce on her prey. Who was she dancing for? There was such power emanating from the woman.

I stood on my stool, up on my toes so as not to miss an instant of such a sublime scene. The dance was bewitching, moving. It felt odd to think that soon I was going to leave all of this behind, for a culture that was the opposite, where being a woman required submission and obedience. I was going to have to adapt, probably more than I thought.

The next day, on the boat, we watched impatiently as the African continent drew near. Already the sun seemed different there. We smiled, we were happy, giddy. I was on the verge of fulfilling my childhood dream: seeing Africa, discovering that ancestral soul. I was attracted to how different I imagined the northwest countryside of Africa would be from urban North America. I liked the idea that nature could provide for all my needs. For me, the beauty of nature was perfect, much more so than anything created by humankind. How could we have invented the setting sun, or flowers that bloom into such sweet fruit?

The idea of going back to the roots of humanity made me dream. Was it the ancestral continent, where we think human life began, that beckoned? What stories might Africa and its people share with me? I imagined myself dancing, carried away by the sound of drums like the heartbeat of the earth.

I was looking for authenticity. I had been dreaming of African colors and flavors for so long. My senses were on high alert.

The Dancer

SEPTEMBER 27, 2019
284th day in captivity

The dancer unroped her sails,
Loosed images dwindled in shadow.
Amid the gathered stars she twinkled away
And swayed the darkness to and fro.

Her veil swelled toward the sky,
Caught the light with every toss of her head.
The dance lasted an instant, and eternity
Brushed against her as it ebbed . . .

On her fingers, music
Snapped and twirled through the air,
Tangled in her plumes of silk
And dropped to the floor.

Music unbound
In her thrumming feet—
The dancer is pure sound
And she dreams the dance of the free.

[3]

Chaos

CARS CAREENED PAST each other in the streets of Casablanca—carelessly, at least to my eyes as a Canadian. I'd already experienced this kind of traffic before, in Latin America, an organized chaos that its participants navigated so nonchalantly. How do people make sense of such confusion? I would never have had the nerve to drive in this kind of anarchy. I watched women making their way through the traffic with infants dangling from their backs. I had the urge to get out of the car and place the babies in a position that was more familiar and comfortable to me, head up and feet down. But the children seemed secure, dreaming away as the mothers strode about confidently.

The hubbub amused me. I was laughing, and admiring Luca, who wove in and out of the traffic like a salmon leaping up a waterfall. And all without nicking a single bumper!

"See," he told me, "you used to criticize my driving in Italy, you told me I was nuts, but now it's awfully convenient that I know how to drive in such a mess!"

He was calm, almost regally so, skirting around the cars that came at us like rabid scrap heaps. The car plowed on, in and out of every curve, sauntering blithely in the midst of the blaring horns, the cacophony assaulting our ears. Luca had the situation under control.

We had just arrived in Morocco, and already I could tell that Luca would take us to Togo without breaking a sweat. Perfect! I couldn't have asked for a better traveling companion. He would drive, and I'd sit tight as co-pilot. I didn't have his skills, and my sense of direction had always left something to be desired.

"But I have other qualities," I reminded him with a smile.

ROADS AND LANDSCAPES flew by under the African sun, beaming and blinding on the steel blue of the car. The light painted the car beautifully as we drove through this vast continent of a thousand shimmering stories and histories.

After over nine hundred miles in Morocco, our little car, with Luca still at the wheel, had become expert in the art of avoiding obstacles. We were inseparable—the car, Luca, and me. We drove across the last stretches of asphalt, our car inching along among donkeys, luxury cars, and countless rusting vehicles. As we got closer to Mauritania, the tension started to feel palpable.

At one point we entered a land that belonged only to itself, where no laws applied. We were both somewhere and nowhere, crossing the two-and-a-half-mile stretch of sand between Morocco and Mauritania, a realm of dust where there are still a few landmines buried, and where we came across the carcasses of cars, hundreds of them, stripped down; they hadn't survived the ordeal of no-man's-land.

What a perplexing place. There was no government, no roads, and no rules. We drove slowly, following a car far ahead of us which in turn was following in the tracks of the previous vehicle. If that car didn't get stuck in the sand, then we could pass. If it didn't trip a mine, we had nothing to worry about. It was testing the terrain for us. We weren't the first to cross this hostile strip, of course: anyone who crosses the border has to pass through that one route. All things considered, the risks were probably pretty low. But the arid, post-apocalyptic landscape was no less eerie.

We'd heard about this infamous no-man's-land, where all manner of contraband passed through. People warned us about the
area as if they were recounting an ancient legend around a fire at
nightfall, the sparks casting sinister shadows. It's a tale that sends
shivers down your spine: blurry, foggy with misunderstandings.
Now, we had no trouble understanding why.

The car in front of us seemed to have triumphed. Now it was
our turn. A little farther on, the first Mauritanian traders came
running toward us, announcing the end of the disputed territory.
The ghostly landscape gave way to a stunning human throng. Our
white skin flashed that there was money to be made, and men
wearing the traditional boubou chased the car, waving wares for
sale or else hoping for foreign currency, wanting to do business
with us.

A World Condemned

Under the stars, the sky cracks open,
Fissures spider and curl
As rivulets of rain fall
And wash over the uncertain world.

The sky is wrong, it's tangled and torn
And nothing is what it was before.
That morning I watched a world broken,
Swathed in the clouds, in the storm.

The desert was a shelter, so peaceful
But now the sands have turned.
They conjure a frightened people
Who want to but cannot run.

So the universe collapses ...
I am trapped in shattered light.
Stars are spinning, bursting like glass
And sparks rain over a wasted earth.

The wind snares in land's sharp edge,
Panicked and wild to shake loose.
Roaring, unruled, it rages,
Whistles and tugs at my clothes.

I gasp, I leap
To catch the stars hurtling by.
But the ground crumbles as I step
Into the slip of time.

[4]

The Frenchman

THE WINDOW ON the passenger side framed the light as if it were the most beautiful work of art. Seen from this angle, the sun looked even redder, more dazzling. I admired its slow drop toward the horizon, as if it were wrapped in the powerful colors of the fading day. Vibrant shades of red radiated inside the enormous sphere, giving the impression that it was growing bigger. I was hypnotized. Beams of light stretched to the end of the sand like long arrows that seared through our bodies as they tried to reach the end of the horizon. The fiery colors clung delicately to three little clouds that ambled across the sky just then, at just the right moment. We came up to the border slowly. The broken roads delayed us a little, but we hoped to reach the end of Mauritania with the setting sun.

At the border, darkness was spreading already, surrounding us, prowling around the car we had just parked while we filled out the necessary paperwork to continue our journey. We weren't yet adept at calculating African time. On this continent, the course of the day is different; the hours are longer, drawn out.

For instance, we had no idea how long it would take to fill out the car's insurance papers. A man in his mid-thirties clumsily held a flashlight between his chin and shoulder to light his typewriter.

He had a hard time directing the weak, flickering beam onto the keys. All at once he plucked out three or four letters in a row. At last, things seemed to be moving a bit.

In the distance, a TV set, which must have been connected to a battery since there was no electricity on the border, was broadcasting a soccer game. Five or six people sat on the floor, their faces barely lit by the screen. Luca got up to stretch his legs while the insurance man continued his laborious task. Curious, Luca headed toward the TV to watch the game: Italy happened to be playing. Meanwhile I stayed, sending good vibes to the insurance man, secretly encouraging him. I wished he would finish his work before nightfall.

"How's it going?" Luca came back to check in.

"He's not done yet," I replied, discouraged.

Once the papers were finally filled out, we were told that the border was closed for the night, so we couldn't enter Mali right away anyway. We found a little corner out of the way, and we set up our tent. A boy came up to us.

"Come join us if you want to eat or drink something. We're over there, by the fire."

Around the fire, we met a French man, an interesting fellow who, since his youth, had had many adventures in Africa. He now lived in Burkina Faso with his wife, and he invited us to visit them if we ever passed through Bobo-Dioulasso. He used to travel this way regularly to visit his family in France. He told us that if we didn't have time to reach a town to spend the night, we could stop in any village to ask for permission to pitch our tent there. He did it all the time, and the village chiefs seemed to appreciate the visits. The man loved African culture. The people here were warm, he assured us. He was the expert, and we listened to his stories and took his advice to heart.

[5]

The Village

THE SUN WAS once again starting its downward journey, and once again we were moving too slowly. There were giant potholes scattered along the roads, slowing us down. We had two options: either take the track in the bush that ran alongside the asphalt road, or deke around on the road, which was completely rutted. They weren't potholes, they were craters! Sikasso was the next town on our way, but we wouldn't get there until nightfall. I watched Luca steering diligently, carefully, back and forth between the road and the bush. Most of the time the track was in better condition than the road. The sun was fading in the distance. I remembered what the Frenchman had said around the fire, and suggested to Luca that we find a safe place to sleep.

"Do you want us to stop at a village?" He was concentrating.

"Yes, I think I'd like that."

Turning briefly to me, Luca nodded with a smile. It was decided, then. I was excited at the idea of staying with locals for the night and learning a little more about their culture.

"Look!" Luca was pointing to a wooden sign, with the name of a village engraved by hand. It's five miles away, he added, pretty far in. "Do you still want to go?"

Of course I wanted to go! I was a bit embarrassed to impose, to be inviting ourselves to the village, but at the same time I was so curious. And to tell the truth, I didn't want to drive all the way to Sikasso at night.

Luca branched off onto what looked like a path. Squinting, he tried to ignore the sound of branches scratching the body of his poor car. The path got narrower and narrower as we made our way through the bush. Finally, at the end of the five miles, which seemed endless, we saw a pretty little hamlet. We waved hello to the first villagers we passed, and then stopped as a crowd gathered around us.

"Hello! Would it be possible to talk to the village chief?" Luca asked a young man who seemed intrigued by our presence.

No answer. That is, no answer we could understand, since the villagers spoke a dialect that we couldn't make out. It didn't seem to be Bambara, the language spoken by most Malians.

"Does anyone speak French?" Luca asked as he got out of the car.

Despite my embarrassment, I was throwing *hellos* all around, waving to all the beautiful people. Good thing Luca isn't shy, I thought; nothing fazes him.

Luca looked at me quizzically.

"What do we do? I think they're going to get the chief." He pointed to a few villagers who were walking away.

"Let's wait," I replied. "I think they're waving at us to wait."

A few minutes later, the village chief came to welcome us.

"*Parlez-vous français?*" Luca asked.

He gestured no, and showed us something in the distance.

"I think he's trying to tell us that someone else is coming," I said.

I confess that I had a moment of doubt as the chief and the other men signed and waved. They spoke a language unknown to us, lived differently than we did, didn't use the same hand gestures—how could we manage to understand each other? But finally, after some time, we heard the voice of someone who spoke a language we knew well.

"*Bonsoir!* Welcome to our village. How can we help you?"

The voice belonged to a slender young man.

"I'm sorry it took me so long to get here, I was in the neighboring village. I am the only one here who speaks French."

Luca told him that we were looking for a safe place where we could pitch our tent for the night. The young man explained the situation to the chief, who gave us a wide, welcoming smile, and pointed us to the center of the village. The presence of the translator put me at ease. What luck that we could speak with one of the villagers! He seemed delighted with our impromptu visit. The Frenchman was right: they were welcoming and warm.

The women got to work: one was heating water for us to bathe, while others started cooking. The various preparations were underway, and the chief invited us to sit with him in front of his hut, around the fire, with his brother and the translator.

The chief's wife appeared a little later, carrying a large bowl of millet with a delicious ginger sauce. She didn't eat with us, instead heading back to the other women. We all ate with our hands from the same bowl. Luca and I, wanting to do things right, imitated the chief and the other guests. We didn't know their customs, and didn't want to offend them by making a mistake. We knew it was a great privilege to eat with the village leaders. We spent a pleasant evening, with fascinating, constructive exchanges. There were many questions on both sides.

At one point, Luca pointed out a few constellations to the chief, who seemed interested. He got up and grabbed a pen and a piece of paper to draw the stars of Orion.

We learned from the translator that the villagers spoke Senoufo, a dialect of the Sikasso region. We drank tea and the conversation went on until late in the evening. We finally went to bed, weary from the long day. We'd never been so happy to crawl into our tent!

The next morning, the chief invited us to have breakfast before we set off again. These people, though poor, were overwhelmingly generous. They shared what little they had with us, with open, sincere smiles.

Thinking back to the little piece of paper on which the chief had drawn the stars, I wanted to give him a gift, to show our gratitude. In the car, I had a nice new notebook and multicolored ballpoint pens. I gave him the pens and the notebook, and he thanked me effusively. Everyone seemed delighted, and I was glad. What moving humanity, and what a lovely encounter.

I was thankful again to our French friend for having suggested that we experience it.

[6]

Mistake

LUCA AND I had transit visas to Burkina Faso. We would rather have had short-stay visas, which were valid for ninety days, but they were too expensive. So we had three days, just enough time to cross the country to reach Togo. We were disappointed that we couldn't stay longer, but we had to manage our money carefully.

We hadn't forgotten the Frenchman's offer. In Bobo-Dioulasso, Luca gave him a call.

"Perfect, we'll be there in a few minutes," I heard him say before he hung up.

We spent a lovely evening in the company of the man and his wife. We danced a lot, and drank a lot. Our host told us that evening about a special visa, the common visa of the Entente territories, which is valid in five countries—Benin, Burkina Faso, Togo, Ivory Coast, and Niger. It was fairly affordable, and might allow us to stay longer in Burkina Faso. We had to give it a try!

The next morning we thanked our kind hosts and left for the capital, Ouagadougou. We were hoping to get the Entente visa at the Direction du contrôle des migrations, but the official there was a sour man.

"You only have a transit visa, so go through, and get out of the country," he said.

The detour to Ouagadougou had cost us precious time, and our visa expired that same evening. We had to make a decision.

"Instead of going to Togo right away," I said, "why don't we go to Benin?"

I don't know where the idea came from. Luca looked at me, perplexed.

"Do you want to go to Benin?"

"I don't want to stop right now, I want to see the country. My uncle said Benin is worth the trip."

"If that's what you want, we can go spend Christmas on a beach in Benin and join our Togolese friend after the holidays."

Luca seemed to have a headache. Maybe it was the effect of our drunken night.

Usually, we checked border security well before going anywhere. We were wary, and always on our guard. But we had to leave Burkina Faso in a few hours. We were pressed for time, so we didn't stop, try to find Wi-Fi, check out the state of the border.

Big mistake. This one misstep was going to lead us straight to trouble.

At the last checkpoint before the border with Benin, the two guards asked us peculiar questions. Were we hiding guns in the trunk of the car? One of the policemen laughed, as if it were a joke. Luca simply replied that we were not, but they still searched the car from top to bottom.

"It's okay, you can go," they said finally, and sent us on our way.

The road to Benin was in horrible shape too. It looked like the road to the Senoufo village. We were crawling along, slaloming around again to avoid losing a tire. The sun was still dipping, dipping toward the horizon. Time was running out, time was slowing down.

The trap was near.

PART II

The Mujahideen

CAPTIVITY: DAY 1 TO DAY 16

Shivers

Something crept up, I saw
Someone in my way
In the night's desolate maw...
I saw it—there!—stealing away.

The presence was uncanny.
Who would try to strike fear,
Send shivers through my body?
Who would dare come so near?

I moved a little and stopped.
What evil did the shadow mean?
I see you, I shouted, my throat in a knot.
You won't come for me!

Before me the trail shifted and quaked,
Thrusting up trees.
This strange forest was my fate,
The earth cracking under my feet.

I heard laughter, a gasp
In the fog, a woman in chains.
I screamed for a future I couldn't grasp
And stood rooted, unmoving again.

[7]

Ambush

DECEMBER 17, 2018.

There was something in the air, as if the universe was trying to get our attention, warning us that something was wrong. Luca was so jittery he could hardly sit still. The tension was palpable, electric. The mood in the car was heavy, imposing, disturbing.

We were going barely twelve miles an hour, no faster. We were crossing part of the W National Park, also known as the elephant park. The road here too was a wreck, and it was hard to maneuver the car. As night fell we got even jumpier. The border with Benin must have been at least thirty miles away.

We saw a truck parked on the side of the road, with two men on board. Luca stopped to ask them if the road was any better up ahead. One of the men, without getting out of the truck, told him, yes, we would soon find that the road improved. We thanked him and drove away.

About three miles farther on, a scene was sketched out against the sky—frozen, static. The road got suddenly darker, and my blood ran cold. Six men in turbans were waiting for us, armed with Kalashnikovs. The scene filled the whole space. I will never forget how Luca and I looked at each other right then, sharp, a warning; a glance loaded with meaning, eviscerating. Had we reached the end of our trip? Were we going to die here? Our fate hung in the air, brushing past each Kalashnikov, each of the men who held us in their sights.

Four of them leapt at Luca, shouting words we couldn't understand in Bambara. They pointed their guns at him, looking for all the world like madmen, with nothing to lose. I was spared, at least a little: the other two men opened the car door and gestured with the barrel of their Kalashnikovs. Our assailants were less afraid of women, apparently. They made us back up, away from the road and into the forest, where they motioned for us to sit down and be quiet.

I looked at Luca again—another shared glance I will always remember, full of uncertainty. Were we going to survive? I had broken out into a cold sweat; I felt dizzy from the unimaginable possibilities racing through my mind. I was scared, but I had to keep hold of myself. Luca took my hands in his to reassure me. We could hear the strained voices of our captors, a tumble of words that made no sense to us. We watched and listened, tried to assess the situation, to understand.

A young man came up to us. He spoke French.

"We've been waiting for you. We were told an Italian and a Canadian were coming in a blue car. You took a long time!"

He then ordered Luca to get on a motorbike a little ways off. Luca gripped my hands.

"She's my wife," he begged, "she has to come with me. I can't leave her behind! What are you going to do to her?"

Luca was afraid our kidnappers would separate us if they knew we weren't married. The rules around relationships between men and women are strict in the Muslim faith, and Luca didn't want to risk losing me. His whole body was taut. There was no way he wanted to leave me alone with the five other men.

"She has to come with me on the bike," he insisted. "She's my wife. *Elle est ma femme!*"

One of the gang stood apart—the little boss. Luca would call him that because he was clearly an underling, working for a much more important leader. The man who spoke French, whom I called the translator, reported what Luca had said. The little boss calmly signaled to the others that he accepted the request.

The journey seemed to last forever. How many miles did we cover? I have no idea, but we drove on well after dark, zipping ahead on the motorbikes while other men followed in our car, far behind. When we finally stopped, before heading into the W Park, one of the young men unrolled a blanket on the ground for us to sit on while they went to hide our car inside the park. There were no roads in the dense, craggy bush, and I didn't see how the car would make it out in one piece. We never knew exactly where they hid it, or what happened to it after that; we never saw our heroic steed again.

Death

She slipped on her forever dress
And painted herself the color of sky.
With gloves made of darkness
From the ground she took her scythe...

She gathered flowers that wilted too fast,
Eclipsed the moon and hid her trail.
She went to the beasts breathing their last
And kissed the wounded and frail.

She watched life go by unfettered,
Saw it move, bend, go free.
Every day she shared
The other's divine journey.

She put out lights along her path,
Gathered in her body the endless years.
She spoke with souls newly hatched
And whispered secrets beyond their tears.

[8]

Among the
Fula People

THE LITTLE BOSS was pacing back and forth, his phone pressed to his ear. Someone was giving him orders for our trip. The Italian and the Canadian had been captured, and now things were starting to happen. The translator wasn't coming with us. He explained to us before we left that we were going to meet their leader, that it wouldn't take more than three days to get there—the first of many lies we would be told. He said they were muja-hideen, soldiers fighting in the way of Allah. We were supposed to help them in their mission. At the time we didn't fully grasp what he was telling us. We thought we'd been kidnapped by a bunch of second-rate bandits who planned to take us to their chief. Maybe he wanted to steal what little money we had in our bank accounts? We just hoped he wouldn't go after our families.

Three motorbikes were lined up in a row. Meanwhile, members of the group were collecting some things for us: food they had found in the trunk, a pot, our camp stove, and our tent. Luca tried to gesture that my contact lenses and cleaning solution were in the car, but they never managed to make out what he was telling them. I didn't have glasses, which would have been much easier to explain. In any case, at that point my contacts were the least of my worries.

They gave us clothes to wear that were typical of the region—loose tops that went down to our knees and plain cotton pants—but they must have been extra-large and we had to tie them around our waists with string. The tops and the pants matched: mine were purple and Luca's navy blue. They handed us long turbans that we were supposed to wrap around our heads and faces, then sunglasses, gloves, and big overcoats. We were going to melt in these outfits in the 120°F heat. Finally, when not a single patch of white skin was visible, we were ready to go. We had to cross the W National Park to get to the first Fula camp.

The road was rough, and the three bikes were constantly getting caught in elephant tracks, snagging in the wide hollows of their footsteps. The ground was soft and wet and we were sinking all over the place. Our kidnappers didn't seem so professional now; under their turbans, their faces looked very young. But behind those kids there must have been a strong, well-organized command, and the young men diligently took us to their leader.

As we traveled through the park, a breathtaking event unfolded before us. The circle of life and the laws of nature, which can seem cruel, were doing their thing. A big cat streaked by at lightning speed, chasing a gazelle sprinting just ahead. The hunt was terrifying: we could see the legs of both animals stretching heroically, gracefully, blurred with speed. One was running for its life, while the other was tailing lunch. With my heart in my throat, I rooted quietly for the gazelle—for the victim, not the executioner.

In that instant, I could guess at what the poor gazelle must have been going through—exhausted, yet driven by the desire to survive. The chase bounded on far beyond us, and I never did find out how the story ended. I still don't know who won the race.

THE SECOND NIGHT, darkness fell before we were able to reach the first camp. One of the mujahideen stopped and fired a gun in the air—one of their many means of communication. They listened, hoping for an answer from the camp. Luca and I listened too. But there was nothing, only the sound of elephants, though we couldn't see them. We were still far from the camp; we had to set up here.

That night I was woken up with a start by shots in the distance—machine-gun fire, explosions, grenades! Luca was awake too. "War sounds," I whispered. He frowned.

"You're right. If it's from the camp, I'm glad we're not there." He sat up halfway. "Listen! The kidnappers are praying."

I listened. Their voices trembled; they were afraid. We were inside the tent and couldn't see what was happening. Luca glanced outside before coming back to my side.

"I can't see anything," he said, stroking my face a little to reassure me.

Everything was out of our control; we were at the mercy of the men. A gunfight had broken out somewhere nearby and we couldn't do anything about it. I huddled a little closer to Luca. The fighting eventually stopped, and I went back to sleep.

The next morning, Luca left the tent and headed toward the little boss. Signing to make himself understood, he evoked the noises we'd heard during the night, and tried to explain that we didn't want to go any further. The little boss dialed a number on his phone and handed it to Luca. The translator answered. It was nothing, he calmly told Luca, just the Malian army; it was over now. We had to keep going. Luca hung up and gave the phone back to the little boss before turning to me. For the time being, he said, it was better to follow our captors, but the first chance we got we would try to escape. I nodded in agreement.

We arrived at the camp in late morning. We were offered water to wash, and given rice with mutton. I had been a vegetarian for over five years. Many things would change after a few months of captivity, and malnutrition would shift my principles, but that day I was still holding on to my vegetarianism.

The little boss greeted his acolytes, who were preparing to return to their camp. We didn't know it yet, but our epic motorbike trek with the Fulani would last about twenty days—not three, as we had been told. The team would change at each new camp, depending on the area. Only the little boss would remain with us throughout the trip.

After the first week on the road, things had changed. There were more motorbikes; the teams seemed to pair up, and never left. All the men were going to meet the leader, we'd been told. By the end of the trip, our caravan had about fifteen motorbikes. Thirty men, and one woman: me.

Since I was dressed and turbaned like a man in order not to be noticed, newcomers to the group greeted me—Fulani men greet each other, but not women. There was always a moment of awkwardness when they realized that I was a woman, since it's forbidden for strict Muslims to look at another man's wife. It made for some embarrassing moments for them, but to me it made them seem more human: these encounters showed me that they were vulnerable too, that even I had the ability to unsettle them.

[9]

The Third Day

WE HAD BEEN riding for three days, and Luca was getting impatient.

"They keep lying to us, they say we're going to meet the leader, but where is he?"

He didn't like being lied to, and he wanted to know what was going on. He decided to investigate.

One of the men in the new group who were in charge of us understood a few words of French. Luca went up to him.

"I've had enough! You say we're about to get wherever we're going, but we never get anywhere! Where are you taking us?"

Luca was so upset he even dared admonish the guy.

"Look at me when I'm talking to you!"

"I don't understand, *je ne comprends pas le français*," the man mumbled, looking at the ground. He was trying to avoid the discussion, but by then it seemed inevitable.

"Yes, you do understand! You all think you're strong with your AK-47s but you won't even look me in the eye. I'm warning you, we're not moving until you tell us the truth. Where are you taking us? To whom?"

The little boss watched the discussion unfold, interested. He didn't understand French, but he knew how to interpret the gestures and expressions of someone who didn't want to follow anymore. The little boss stayed calm; that seemed to be his nature. He handed his phone to Luca and once again we heard the translator's voice. The translator and Luca talked for a while, but it didn't go anywhere. The translator told him to follow the group quietly, that we would arrive at our destination later in the day. Luca finally gave up and we had to get on the bikes again.

A few hours later, I was getting increasingly nervous, and looking desperately for a way out. I was on the lead motorbike with the guide, and Luca was traveling with the little boss in the middle of the group. The gunmen brought up the rear. Unfortunately for me, the guide was a bit of a noodle: no muscle, just one long, overcooked spaghetti. Physical activity isn't part of Fula culture. At home, they prefer to drink tea and chat around the fire.

For some reason, my driver was in more of a hurry than the others. We were zipping across the sand at full speed, far ahead of the pack. But at such high speed it takes a bit of muscle to steer a motorbike skidding constantly in the sand. No matter how much I straightened the handlebars and held the man's arms when I felt the bike skidding, I couldn't always straighten the machine. We actually crashed three times in barely a few hours. The third time he lost control was spectacular: we ran right into the ass end of a donkey, which started braying, and we landed in the sand, the bike above us, prize fools. Luca got off the little boss's motorbike and ran toward me.

"Edith, are you okay? Are you hurt?"

My patience had its limits too. I didn't want to ride with the spaghetti man any longer, I said. Luca, who was as annoyed as I was, made it clear to the little boss that there was no way I would keep riding with the lead. As placid as ever, the little boss reorganized the caravan and placed me at the back with one of the gunmen. I didn't fall off the bike again after that.

Our second day on the bike, I'd had to take out my contact lenses because my eyes were full of sand. It wasn't an easy decision to make; my eyesight is bad, and I knew I wouldn't be able to see much. Without my contacts I felt more vulnerable, but keeping my eyes healthy was more important. My vision was blurry, and I couldn't see the branches coming, so they whipped at my face. Sometimes I could react quickly when I saw my driver duck, but most of the time we had to stop and put my scarf back on after it had caught in the trees and unraveled.

On the third day, we stopped at noon for the Dhuhr prayer and lunch. I saw our chance.

"We have to run away," I told Luca, "otherwise it's over. Now or never."

Poor Luca didn't know what to do. He didn't want to put us in danger, but at the same time he could see that the walls were closing in. He decided to talk to the boy who understood a little French. They talked for a while, and the men started to get worked up. Finally, Luca came back to me. Faltering, he announced that our journey would end in the Sahara.

"You know, the place we're not supposed to go. In the north of Mali."

We knew that northern Mali had been a red zone since the Tuareg uprisings against the Malian state in 2012 and 2013. Luca looked deflated.

"I tried to convince them to let us go, to tell them we wouldn't go into the Sahara with them, but obviously we have no say in any of this."

There, on the third day, was when we really understood what we had stumbled into. We weren't caught up with a bunch of petty thieves, we were in the clutches of a major organization that would ask our governments to pay ransoms for our release, or use us in a prisoner exchange.

I grabbed a few bags of water I had with me and slipped them into my pockets as I began to move away. We had to risk it, we had to try everything to escape.

"We're going," I called to Luca. "Take some water with you too."

A few of the men surrounded us. Luca slipped some bags of water into his coat pockets, and motioned that we were leaving.

There was a commotion. The guide pointed his gun at Luca's head. But my friend wouldn't give in.

"Let us go," he said. "We will not go to the Sahara. If we go there, we're dead!"

He walked back toward me as I continued to walk away slowly. The little boss raised a hand for Luca to stop, then he handed him the phone so that he could talk to the translator again.

"No! I'm done, I have nothing more to say to him. The man tells me nothing but lies!"

The little boss still had his hand up in the air. He gestured to Luca not to move. He gave an order to a young man, who took out a pair of handcuffs and ran toward me. Handcuff the woman first.

My hackles went up, and I could feel the wild beast within me stirring. Instinctively, I ran and hid behind Luca. There was no way I was going to be handcuffed! The young man, obviously inexperienced, was forced to turn to Luca. I grabbed Luca by the wrists and pulled his arms behind his back. They wouldn't handcuff my so-called husband either! In that position, Luca was unable to defend himself; he wasn't going to fight me off to free his arms. From behind him, I was kicking, flailing at nothing to get the young man to back up. Thinking back now, the absurdity of it makes me laugh.

Then, all at once, out of the blue—

"Okay! Stop! It's okay, we'll come with you," Luca said.

"What? Really?" I answered, stunned. I let go of Luca's wrists and he took control of the situation, waving at the man with handcuffs to step back.

Luca turned back to me. He looked shaken.

"For now we have to follow them, whether we like it or not, *principessa*," he said.

He could call me a princess, but I knew Luca was right: confrontation wouldn't get us anywhere. The little boss was satisfied. He didn't want to be forced to handcuff us, because we had to travel as discreetly as possible.

[10]

The Trade

WE'D BEEN RIDING north for almost two weeks. The landscape had shifted from bush to desert, and our kidnappers
struggled to control the motorbikes in the sand. We were among
the Fulani until we had crossed the many streams of a river. We
figured we were probably north of Mopti, in the inner delta of the
Niger River. Everything was well thought out: we traveled through
remote areas so we wouldn't be seen, and crossed the river on
pinasse boats, the canoes used by the local fishermen. There was
a seat in the bow and another in the stern. Fishing nets had been
tossed in the bottom of the boat, and sometimes a few dead fish.

We crossed about twenty branches of the river, and the number and size of the pinasses varied constantly. We could load three
motorbikes on a large boat, but most of the time there was only
one small boat, which could only carry one motorbike and its rider.
Every passage took several hours; good thing Africans tend not to
be in much of a hurry. These men had all the time in the world,
while Westerners are always a little impatient. Here in the delta,
the two worlds collided: for Luca and me, everything seemed to
take forever; we were in a hurry to get to our destination. We didn't
yet know what awaited us, but we hoped that we would soon be
able to get out of this mess. We still had a lot to learn about our
new way of life, and it was hard to get used to.

We passed through isolated villages, each one a clutch of mud huts. Children stared at us while holding jars balanced on their heads, and their mothers looked up from their laundry, both feet in a pool of water, to watch the motorbikes go by. I tried to show them my face, to let them know I was a white woman, subtly letting my scarf slide, as if it was unwinding by mistake. My driver would look at me in the rearview mirror and tell me to pull it up. He must have thought it seemed to be loosening a bit easily, but I wasn't used to wearing a veil, so he didn't seem too surprised. Sometimes I also took off my gloves so that the villagers could see my white hands, and even held my wrists together to let them know that I was being held captive. But what could those poor people do? They were barely getting by as it was, and it would have been far too dangerous to try anything against our captors. The kidnappers avoided contact with civilians as much as possible, though at one point, one of the mujahideen ran over a chicken, and the little boss had to turn back to compensate the village chief for the loss, while the others kept us far enough away.

We always took a break at lunchtime in a bushy, out-of-the-way place. Luca and I prepared a meal while the others prayed. We always kept to ourselves, with the bag that had been prepared for the journey. We still had some of our own food left over from the car our captors had hidden in the park.

The road was endless. We were exhausted. Luca's back ached, and riding on the back of a motorbike wasn't helping. We were thirsty, too. The men offered us water from the Niger River, though we were reluctant to drink the river water. But everything was going to change.

After sixteen days, our adventure with the Fulani was coming to an end.

The sky was bright with twilight, and the sun dipped down, taking some of the day's heat with it. Another group was waiting for us, with a pickup truck hidden under a tree. These men were different: they spoke Arabic, not Bambara. The Fulani would be leaving us in the hands of our new hosts, who were older and seemed more professional, but no friendlier. We hadn't managed to escape the Fulani, and the trap seemed to be closing more tightly.

THE ARABS HAD taken over. They were among the many minions of Iyad Ag Ghaly, leader of JNIM, the Group for the Support of Islam and Muslims, which was founded in 2017 after most of the Malian jihadist groups merged. The men offered us food and milk. They seemed to be waiting for darkness to move us. That night we traveled just a few miles. We only had to go as far as another pickup, which would take us into the desert the next day. We left at daybreak.

The two trucks were racing, chasing each other. We were in the first one with the driver, and five other men were sitting in the back, in the bed, on a tall pile of supplies pinned down under netting. The other truck was similar to ours, but there was a big machine gun mounted on a tripod in the back. The men had larger weapons to make sure we could travel safely into the desert, an area that was more susceptible to attack.

We rode for two days across the sand, whirring up and down the dunes as if they were huge waves. In the desert, people drive at full speed to avoid getting stuck. I felt like I was in the middle of a storm, riding up and down on vast, parched swells. Every inch of our bodies hurt from holding on to whatever we could to avoid smashing our heads against the roof of the cabin.

And so I learned that the only things that move fast in the desert are the cars.

PART III

Into the Desert

CAPTIVITY: DAY 17 TO DAY 24

One Day More

AUGUST 25, 2019
251st day in captivity

The day ambled across the world,
Stretching out the seconds
As it circled the earth
And grazed each hill in the beyond.

Across the sky the sun spilled its colors:
Reds flamed along the lace of pink,
And the moon lit up the dark corners,
A glowing orb bathed in ink.

Night, swollen with ghosts—
A torrent of dreams rushing as it came,
Quiet but sure, cloaking and soft
With shadow as the earth went around again.

[11]

The Man in Blue

THE SECOND TRUCK had just left us. Our kidnappers had managed to get us safely into the desert, and we had entered our new prison of sand. There was nothing around us for miles, nothing but golden sand, twinkling in the blazing sun.

Our driver stopped in front of a small hut that was well camouflaged, the color of the desert. Tall dry grass wove all around and above it so it was almost invisible from a distance. A slender man dressed in a long blue boubou came out. He greeted the driver and sat down with the others in the back of the truck. Who was this mysterious man, armed with a Kalashnikov, hiding in a tiny hut in the middle of the Sahara? With his somewhat suspicious arrival, the dodgy detours began.

Our driver stopped going north, heading off in a new direction. He stopped at a well. In the Sahara, wells are dug for shepherds and nomads who venture into the desert. The driver had parked so that we couldn't see what he was doing. From where we were sitting there was only sand as far as the eye could see, as far as the horizon. The driver was definitely hiding something from us behind the truck. He'd even made sure to turn the mirrors to face the ground before getting out, and one of the men in the back came up and sat in the driver's seat to keep an eye on us.

Once whatever scheming he was up to was over, the driver climbed back in and we headed to another well, about twelve miles away. Again, the same inexplicable game: the driver got out, turned down the mirrors, another man took his place. This time, the whole process lasted a little longer.

About thirty minutes later, the driver came back, completely out of breath. Had he been running? I'd never seen Arabs in the desert run anywhere. He started the truck, and handed us some dates. I didn't know what he had been up to, but at least he had found something to eat.

The journey seemed erratic and disorienting: shadows and sun danced all around us, and I felt like we were going in circles. Before, we had been driving steadily north, but now we were heading east, or west, or even back south. Were our captors looking for something, or someone? Were they trying to hide our tracks? We stopped again several times, always with the driver hiding or looking for something in the sand. We never found out what it was.

At one point I felt the driver stiffen and I tried to make out what he was seeing, but without my contact lenses it was pointless. Luca leaned toward me; there was a truck on a dune in the distance. I could see color and movement. Our driver yanked the steering wheel and sand spun out beneath our wheels. He honked nonstop, spinning up the dunes and then letting the truck slide down the other side while we gained momentum to climb the next dune. It felt like we were at sea, in a storm of swelling sand. It was pretty impressive to see the six men in the back clinging to the heap of supplies. As for the other truck, it seemed to be running away from us. But why? It was obvious that our driver was trying to reach them. The chase ended when we managed to catch up to the other sand surfer, and the truck came to a standstill.

Grabbing his Kalashnikov, our driver got out and headed for the other truck. Now the man who came up to the front to guard us was the man in blue. The way his loose-fitting clothes flapped in the wind made him look even more mysterious. He was watching the scene attentively, and I couldn't help but find him suspicious, even worrisome. Suddenly, without any warning, he leapt into the driver's seat and peeled away with us on board! He slammed his foot down on the gas, glancing in the rearview mirror every two seconds to see if we were being followed. His eyes were bulging out; he looked terrified. I couldn't see if there were still men back there. With a wan smile, I turned to Luca.

"I think he just stole us from our kidnappers."

Luca also hid a smile. The situation was totally beyond us.

"Maybe," he said, "but we don't know if this guy is better or worse than the others."

Our driver, panicked, continued his crazy sprint through the dunes, still glaring in the rearview mirror. We came back to the first well, and he got out of the truck. That's when we realized that the other men were still in the back of the truck! Luca and I waited to see what would happen next; we never knew which way was up with these people. The man in blue, who had disappeared for a moment, came back, out of breath. Another jogger? We got back on the road for a few miles before stopping again. The man in blue got out, grabbed our duffel bag, and tossed it under a tree.

"I think he wants us to eat here," I told Luca.

By now the wind was raging all around us. It was the first time I had tried to cook in a sand squall. Luca ate as best he could, looking a little demoralized. I could hear the crunching of sand in his teeth. So much for our first mashed potatoes *à la* sand. I hadn't yet mastered the art of desert cooking. There had to be a trick to it. In time, I would learn.

A couple of hours later, we heard the sound of a vehicle in the distance. The man in blue didn't look worried this time. The truck stopped and our previous driver got out. He greeted the man in blue with a big smile and turned around to say goodbye to the occupants of the departing truck. We must have looked completely baffled. Luca rubbed his beard.

"He's back."

It was so confusing.

Right away, we got back in the truck to drop the man in blue off in front of his little hut tucked in the heart of the desert, then we headed north with our driver, the other men still clinging to the netting in the back.

And so we left behind the man in blue, alone with his secrets. There were so many questions to which we would never have any answers.

In the Maze

APRIL 12, 2019
116th day in captivity

The exit moves farther the closer I get.
New passages open in the maze.
Burrowing behind, waiting ahead
When the dark lights suddenly blaze.

In the ground I see a shimmering sky.
I fall through clouds of anxious dreams,
The sky lost in the oldest destiny...
But with each step it looks new, it seems...

The labyrinth hides our hopes and tomorrows,
Abandoned memories in the gutter.
I look up with admiration and woe
As the indescribable future blurs.

On the walls, words are everywhere,
Repeating life's every moment.
In the labyrinth's corners I hide my fear
And hold on to the wind's lament.

[12]

The Leader

THE DAY AFTER all the desert intrigue, we pulled up in front of two small tents a few yards apart. As we approached the tent where our bags had been dropped off, we saw American wrappers, containers, and food on the ground. They obviously hadn't come from the desert: we were not the first hostages to pass through here. The men in the back of the truck unloaded all the supplies, on the orders of a man we later nicknamed Parano. The driver looked at us, evidently pleased with himself.

"Welcome to your five-star hotel!" he said in heavily accented French.

The tent was big enough to stand up in, and there was room to move around a little. We didn't yet know that we would never again be housed in such luxury. After the five-star suite, the stars would drop off one by one every time we changed locations.

A few days later, at midday, we heard the bang of a gunshot. Was something about to happen? Was someone signaling his arrival? Sure enough, that evening, a vehicle arrived, carrying a sheep and more supplies. The men cut the animal's throat, and we could hear the sounds of it being butchered. They hung one of the legs, dripping blood, in our hut. There was a lot of movement back and forth.

I watched the hanging, dripping leg.

"We don't have a knife," I said to Luca. "How does he think we're going to cut the meat?"

Luca picked up the leg.

"I'm going to ask them to cut it into pieces."

He left to join in the excitement while I lit a fire. Luca came back with the carved-up shank.

At nightfall, another vehicle drove up. We heard two men talking on the way to our hut—a commander and his interpreter.

"Good evening," the interpreter said. "May we come in?"

Once inside, they shone their flashlight straight at Luca, who squinted and winced, and sat down on the floor. Throughout their whole conversation, they never lowered the lamp, deliberately blinding him.

"Welcome to Al-Qaeda, if I may put it that way."

The two visitors spoke to each other for a few minutes in Arabic before the interpreter turned back to us.

"We would like to ask you a few questions. We need to know your profession, your age..."

Luca answered their questions vaguely. For example, instead of saying he was an architect, he said he worked on the family farm. It wasn't a lie, since he did both, but he wanted to avoid revealing anything that might be of interest.

At the end they said goodbye and left our hut. After the exchange, Luca looked uneasy. After staring at the blinding beam of the flashlight, he must have been seeing stars or geometric shapes flickering in the darkness. Maybe he even saw cuts of lamb going around in circles, who knows.

The next day, at dawn, the commander and his interpreter left after the first prayer. We would leave too, later, but first a man came to ask Luca if we had any health problems. Luca said he had back pain and the man gave him anti-inflammatories.

When the time came for us to go, Parano told us to blindfold ourselves before getting into the truck. Shortly thereafter, we found ourselves in a well-hidden spot among the dunes, where the men built a small shelter of branches, plants, and grass.

Here, we would meet Barbarossa.

Sands of Time

Fingers claw at my face—
The sun is at its brightest
And the wind in its race
Clutches a gold-embroidered vest.

To the east, a pyramid of dust
Where dawn is hidden.
A man fights gusts
For the jacket the wind has taken.

The ground seems to tear,
The sands of time shatter;
The man bends as in prayer
Before time's untold power.

The hourglass tries to flow back
Dragging him into its drought.
Captive time, the loss, the lack—
In this desert there's no way out.

PART IV

The Desert Arabs

CAPTIVITY: DAY 25 TO DAY 76

Nightmare

JANUARY 4, 2020
383rd day in captivity

I climb, stumble, and climb again.
I dive down into my nightmares.
I dry my clothes drenched by the rain
And wring dark drops from my hair.

The wind is strange in this country.
It blows and breathes behind me.
In the night it follows me
Until I am trapped in its body.

I swim and sink into oblivion,
The nightmare grabs me from below.
Between earth and delirium
The abyss sweeps away all I know.

It's raining sorrowful tears.
I run and run against the bleak
Sky almost regretful as it tears
And sluices down where I flee.

I shout against the world, I flail
For an escape that's ever in flux.
The crumbling cliffs I scale
Are as light as towers of dust.

The nightmare whispers in the arid air,
Its looming shadow blinds me.
It watches me run, without a prayer,
Among fragrant flowers of misery.

[13]

Barbarossa

LUCA AND I were huddled under our temporary shelter, a large beige sheet supported by four branches—just enough to protect us from the sun while we waited for whatever was to come.

A pickup truck we'd never seen before pulled up and stopped in front of us. Parano waved us aboard. We put our bag in the back, where three armed men and three children were sitting on some supplies. I was stunned: the children looked like they were in their early teens. Tiny soldiers holding outsized rifles. What a cruel place.

Luca opened the passenger door and we climbed in. The new driver gave me the creeps; I felt an immediate, instinctive disgust. He looked fairly old, though he might have been fifty-five or seventy, it was hard to tell. His features were stern and hollow, and his skin was burned, badly damaged by the desert sun. I think he must have been a white Arab, but his skin had turned so brown it was almost black. He was in fact a tricolored man: he had the skin of a Black man, but the features of a white man, and, oddly enough, his salt-and-pepper beard was reddish, as if it had been hennaed at some point.

This disturbing man, who swerved between the dunes like a desert cowboy, was the leader of the new group, all the rest of whom were hanging on for dear life in the back. Now and again, the driver stuck his head out of the window to shout to his men in Arabic. There was nothing gentle about him. His intense, negative energy gave me goosebumps.

He stopped the pickup suddenly and pointed to the place where his men were to build our next shelter. The men and the boys set to work while he lay back in the sand like a pasha, Kalashnikov in hand, shouting out conflicting orders, at once aggressive and flippant. I was dumbfounded.

We would stay with Barbarossa for a month and a half, and the only time we didn't hear him hollering was when he was taking a nap.

When he was asleep, at last, we could hear the desert breathing.

Dentone

THE CHILD SOLDIERS were apprenticing. Barbarossa and the two other adults were mentors to them during the time the group was guarding us. They read the Quran, recited surahs, and learned to bake bread in the sand, to cook pasta, rice, mutton and goat, to slaughter animals and preserve the meat. But not everyone mastered the technique of drying meat, and there were often maggots. The group was allowed two sheep or two goats per month, so the meat of each animal had to last two weeks.

The day of slaughter was a feast for them, and to Luca and me they left the offal—the lungs, liver, heart, and kidneys. Occasionally, they would offer ribs and pieces of meat cooked over the embers. For the first three days after the slaughter there was fresh meat, and after that, dried meat. By the end of the second week, meals consisted of casings stuffed with fried fat.

It took me three months to give up my vegetarianism. In the end I decided it was okay because the animals were treated with respect, and we ate everything that was edible. There was no waste. The cuts I liked least were fried fat, sheep's anus, and tripe. I think the desert Arabs didn't like the anus either, because somehow it always ended up on my plate. The meat was stiff, almost impossible to chew.

The children were also learning how to disassemble Kalashnikovs, clean them, and put them back together. They were taught how to build and camouflage shelters, and how to ride camels. Luca and I had to keep quiet and not wander too far from our shelter. Not doing anything all day was hard. It's not easy to learn to live in limbo, to watch time go by without being able to change things. If at least I'd had a pen and paper, I could have kept my mind occupied. At this stage of our captivity, we still had relative freedom, but I didn't realize it, and I certainly didn't think our situation could get any worse. We still had the right—the privilege— to leave our shelter, to make a fire, prepare our meals. You don't realize what you have until you've lost everything. We thought we had already crossed the border into disaster, unaware of the other disasters that were waiting patiently for us, lurking in the shadow of our destiny.

One of the guards had a significant dental deformity, and Luca nicknamed him Dentone (it's especially effective in Italian!). He had horse teeth, which protruded outrageously out of his mouth. At first I thought that the man had a deep aversion to white people, but when I came to understand Islam better, I realized that he actually disliked unbelievers; that is, those who aren't Muslims and who don't believe in Allah, their god, or Mohammed, their prophet. He always looked at us with disgust in his eyes. The slightest of his gestures betrayed his contempt. He threw our things at us instead of giving them to us or placing them in front of us. He behaved like a brute. One day, Luca got tired of his attitude, and through hand gestures he made Dentone understand that he found him rude. Seething, his face twisted by the insult, Dentone went to find Barbarossa, who was yelling at someone, as usual, for one reason or another.

Shortly afterwards, the two men returned to our shelter. Gesticulating, Barbarossa asked Luca what the problem was. We obviously couldn't have an extensive conversation, since Barbarossa only knew about ten words of French, including *monsieur, madame, manger, hélicoptère, chef, libre, oui,* and *non.*

"*Pas libres,*" Luca said; we were not free. Barbarossa, looking grim, replied, "*Oui, libres,*" while signaling that we could leave the shelter as we pleased.

He was right, we were still free.

Dentone had been taken down a peg, but now he hated us openly. Thank goodness there was a third man besides Barbarossa and Dentone. We had nicknamed him Kindly. He wasn't actually particularly nice, but compared to his buddies, he was okay.

Later that day, I went to wash discreetly behind a clump of grass while Luca lit a fire to cook some pasta. While I crouched, undressing, a bang from the camp startled me. I put down the soap and the water bottle and got dressed in a hurry. Barbarossa was striding toward me. He was fuming, and his crimson face matched his thick beard. He pointed to our shelter with his machine gun and nudged me with the barrel to make me walk faster. Luca was still in front of his fire.

"Did you hear that, Luca? There was a gunshot!"

"I know. The old man shot between my feet."

"What? He's nuts! What did you do?"

"He doesn't want me to cook my macaroni."

Barbarossa didn't want to talk, and he kept pushing me with his gun to shove me into the hut. Dentone laid grass and branches in front of the door so I couldn't get out. I was trapped inside, and Luca was outside with the two maniacs! I peered through gaps in the tent to see what was happening.

The two men told Luca to lean against the wall. Barbarossa was still threatening him with his Kalashnikov. Luca couldn't understand what they wanted. Was he in danger? If so, what was I supposed to do? How should I react? I didn't know what to do.

Suddenly, a knife pierced the canvas. The blade went in and out, up and down and right and left, cutting an opening opposite the door they had just blocked with grass and branches. Barbarossa's face appeared in the hole. He was watching me with a flinty look.

"Luca, are you okay?" I asked quickly, looking over Barbarossa's shoulder.

"Yes, I think they're calming down."

What baffling business.

Barbarossa and Dentone made Luca understand that he could now cook his pasta, then they went back to their own tent.

What had just happened? It was only the first of many ludicrous episodes we would experience with Barbarossa. Maybe he wanted to show us that he was boss, who knows. Barbarossa was a difficult man to understand, and now that Dentone had a grudge against Luca, we couldn't expect any special treatment.

[15]

Flight of
the Mujahideen

FOR A WEEK we had been hearing drones flying day and night. The noise sounded like an airplane, but we knew that wasn't it: airplanes don't go around in circles, searching. They were definitely drones. They seemed to be getting closer and closer to where we were. I kept looking for them in spite of my poor eyesight, hoping to spot something in the sky, but we couldn't see anything.

The men were starting to get tense. We were told to stay inside our tent to avoid being spotted. They didn't come out of their tent too often either. The little freedom we'd had a few days earlier was gone. Going outside was forbidden. Barbarossa called the drones helicopters. I'm not sure that the mujahideen who were keeping us captive knew exactly what drones were, but they were extremely afraid of them. They had a real phobia of what they called helicopters.

The evening before we had to flee, we hadn't been able to eat because fire was now forbidden. In the morning we could hear the drones coming closer and closer. Kindly had been assigned to watch over us. He leaned against the wall near the entrance to our tent, with orders to fire on us if the French army (who were running Opération Barkhane) tried to rescue us. He stayed there for most of the morning.

Barbarossa appeared and sent Kindly back to the others. The boss was now watching over us, which seemed like a bad sign. Usually he left it to his subordinates to guard us, as if it were a trifling task, but that day he stayed crouched like a soldier lurking in his trench, the rifle loaded and his finger on the trigger. From inside the tent we watched him quietly; it was better not to make any sudden moves, nothing that might startle him. After an hour, he waved to us not to move, that he would be back. Obviously we weren't going to move! Under the circumstances we had no desire to toy with his nerves. Barbarossa was in the middle of a war.

He came back with a walkie-talkie and pointed his finger at me. "*Madame!*"

He pointed to my shoes and I understood that I had to put them on right away. I got busy while Barbarossa tore off a piece of the fabric that covered our shelter. Luca stiffened.

"Where are you taking her? We have to stay together, you can't separate us!"

Luca had spoken in French, a language Barbarossa couldn't understand. The old man ignored him, ordered me to move forward, and covered me with canvas from head to toe. Then he pointed to Kindly, who was waiting for me in the distance, a silhouette on the sands flickering in the fumes of the torrid, intensifying heat. It was late morning; it must have been ten o'clock. I took one last look at Luca, who was distraught, and I began to follow Kindly. Another man, whom I had never seen before, joined us. We later nicknamed him the Stranger.

With Kindly in front, and me and the Stranger behind, we fled on foot into the desert, three silhouettes wrapped in canvas, trailed by our shadows across a sea of burning sand. We walked for a long time among the dunes. Our silhouettes shortened until they almost disappeared under our fleeing bodies, then lengthened and finally faded toward the horizon. This journey, as we fled from the drones, seemed to last an eternity. Kindly made me hide

in every patch of dry grass we came across. We had to protect ourselves from the shrieking sun and we tried to share the patches of
dappled, almost non-existent shade. The two men took advantage
of these breaks to listen for the noise of the drones and to guess
at their distance. Sometimes, when they thought the noise was
getting dangerously close, they told me to crouch, and covered me
with the canvas.

At one point we saw two acacias in the distance—exactly what
the men were looking for. There was about fifty feet between the
trees. We could rest there. They would be watching me. They gestured to me to go hide under one acacia tree, and they settled
under the other. I sat under the tree for a good hour, worrying
about Luca, wondering what had happened to him. In the hands
of such unpredictable people, anything was possible. Suddenly, I
heard a voice. It sounded like Barbarossa, but without my contact
lenses I couldn't see anything.

I had already gotten used to the desert and the blurry outlines
of the men, but from time to time it would have been crucial for
me to have good eyesight, to understand what was going on or
what was being asked of me. For example, right then, one of the
two men stood up to wave his arms. Who was he trying to signal?
Them? Me, or someone approaching from the other side of the
dune? Was he waving at the voice I'd heard? Was I supposed to go
to them? Why was he getting so upset? Should I stay, or move? He
kept waving, so I got up and started walking to him, squinting to
try to see better. He became even more agitated, and I froze, not
knowing if I was supposed to move forward or back.

Sand started to fly, spraying up like a fountain. The man must
have been kicking at the sand. That seemed clearer to me, and I
decided to go back under my tree and stay there; if they wanted
me, they could come get me. The sand stopped flying; the fountain
dried up.

A few minutes later, I saw two blurs appear at the top of the
dunes, bright spots that were descending toward us under the

blazing sun. Desert people love brightly colored clothes. I thought there might have been camels, too. I squinted again . . . Yes, camels. I sat down under the acacia tree.

Two newcomers detached themselves from the group and approached me. They motioned for me to get up and follow them. But had I understood their gestures properly? I wasn't sure, but I got up and followed them.

And then, sweet gift from heaven, I heard a tender, familiar voice in the distance.

"Edith!"

I turned and smiled.

"Luca."

I wondered which of the blurry figures was my friend. One of them was coming toward me, and I recognized his gait. With immeasurable joy, I walked toward Luca.

"You're all right, Edith? You're okay?"

I nodded.

"I had to run away with Dentone and one of the kids." He looked annoyed.

Their own journey must have been rough! Still smiling, I handed him my bottle of water without a word and he drank it in one gulp. He was dehydrated. Dentone hadn't given him much water during the long hours of walking in the hot desert sun. I was happy to find him safe and sound. He was smiling at me too.

We continued on our way with the group, which now included about ten men, until we reached an area that was slightly more concealed, a safer place where we could take a break. Dentone then set off in search of grasses, shrubs, and branches to make us a prison. While we were sequestered, they would take some time to rest, cook, and pray, and figure out how to proceed.

At dusk, a man arrived with a dozen camels. Dentone gave us a blanket: from December to March, it gets cold in the desert. The contrast between day and night is intense, and the temperature can drop to freezing. The blanket was too small for the two of us, and we fell asleep on top of each other trying to cover ourselves properly and warm up. We were exhausted.

Dentone woke us up in the night by throwing a bowl of food at us—bread fried in fat with honey. We hadn't eaten since the day before, so we were starving, and devoured everything. Once the meal was finished, seven or eight men left on camels and we stayed with Dentone, Kindly, the Stranger, and two camels. One of the animals would carry the supplies, while the other would take me and Luca. We left shortly after the other group, under the full moon, and walked until the men found a place to set up another camp: two acacias, not too far from each other.

The acacia is a tree that can live in difficult conditions, withstanding extremely high temperatures and low humidity. It can grow in regions that get only one and a half inches of rain a year and with high evaporation rates. The roots run very deep into the ground, with the main root thrusting down two hundred feet to reach the water table. Acacias are a desert tree through and through, with almost straight, whitish thorns over two inches long arranged in pairs at the base of the leaves. We literally slept on a bed of thorns, because it was impossible to sweep them all away; they were everywhere. There is nothing soft in the desert; everything is rough, wild, twisted, barbed.

Luca and I hid for two weeks under the acacia tree, waiting for Barbarossa to return. In his absence, Dentone was in charge. We were almost glad when Barbarossa came back, because we were finally going to be able to move around. And all in all, he was nicer than Dentone. We took our blanket and water jug and followed Barbarossa to the truck that was hidden a few dunes away, leaving behind our prickly home.

Nomads

AUGUST 26, 2019
252nd day in captivity

They walk in a line
Beneath the blazing sun,
As amused shadows trickle down their spines—
Mimics that won't be outdone.

The nomads' shadows peel away
In search of forgotten freedom.
Across the sand in mischievous play
They leave the men whose steps bound them.

A line is drawn on burning sands,
A sunbeam's arrow charred
And sinewed out, far away, rippling and
Stretching into the spectacular.

The freed shadows climb all around,
Striking poses in graceful fledge.
They join the horizon,
A thin, blustering thread.

The nomads go on among the dunes,
And one by one turn to statues of sand.
From the sun they came to rest under the moon
Where their shadows have fled the land.

[16]

The Fast

BARBAROSSA HAD CHOSEN a new location in the desert to build us a shelter. The orders now were not to leave our hiding place except to go to the toilet nearby. Our hideout was so small that Luca and I couldn't sit up straight; our necks and backs were bent and our legs stuck out. Dentone warned us: we had to bend our limbs and hold them inside to be totally invisible. But there were limits, after all; as far as we were concerned, if they really wanted us to stay hidden, they could just build us a larger shelter. So we just didn't listen. If we couldn't sit down, couldn't we at least stretch our legs and lie down comfortably? They ended up covering our legs with my old beige blanket. Now we were well hidden and a little more comfortable. Still, our hideout was tiny, exactly the same width as our two bodies side by side. It was awful. In the end we had to shelter there all day long for several weeks.

It's amazing how time can expand to the point of becoming unbearable when you can't move. I felt trapped, like I was inside a too-narrow hourglass overheating in the blazing sun. I contemplated each grain of sand falling one by one in slow motion, wishing with all my heart that they would fall faster. How do you explain the emptiness you feel when you can no longer do anything at all? When all you do is stare endlessly at the roof of your cramped hiding place? Sometimes the time seemed to pass a little faster if I closed my eyes. One day, just to do something other than stare at the low ceiling, I turned to Luca.

"Do you want to play a game? Ask me questions to try to guess the word I'm thinking of."

Luca stared at me for a second before asking his first question.

"Is it alive?"

"No."

"Does it have a color?"

"No."

"Is it a material object?"

"No."

"Is it transparent?"

"No."

He asked me one question after another, until finally he gave up.

"But Edith, I don't get it. How is it even possible?"

"The word is nothing!"

"What? How was I supposed to guess that? You have to think of words like sun, sand, camel. Not nothing! Nothing doesn't exist!"

"Yes, it does!"

I smiled at him, proud that I'd managed to distract him for a little while.

After a few days, we were getting pretty fed up with the demands of our kidnappers. We couldn't mentally survive this idleness any longer; we had to act. We had to keep our minds busy; we had to fight, to survive! Like the gazelle who had struggled so hard, even though its chances of escaping the lion were small. The drones were still flying around in the sky, and our mujahideen were still on edge.

"What can we do? What if we stop eating? Do you think then they would react?"

Maybe they would negotiate more quickly if they were afraid of losing their merchandise—and by merchandise, I meant us.

"I don't want to sit here and do nothing," I said to Luca.

At that time I was still naïve. We'd been held hostage for only two months, and we didn't understand yet. I thought, or at least I hoped, that I could change the situation. I hadn't yet grasped the magnitude of the mess we were in, the dilemma we faced. I felt that we were getting bogged down; we had to try something.

Luca thought for a moment.

"I don't want to just sit around either. But Edith, you know that if we go on a hunger strike, I won't stop until we get results."

Luca is a stubborn, persistent man. When he spoke these words, I knew that we would fast like fighters, until we fell.

"Are you sure you want to try?"

Of course I did; I was desperate. Our scope of action was limited, and fasting was one thing we could do. The men couldn't force us to eat. The other possibility was to try to escape, but that seemed more dangerous.

"Let's try the hunger strike to start with?"

Luca gazed at me seriously.

"Edith, are you sure this is what you want?"

My mind was made up.

"Yes. I don't want to eat their food anymore anyway, I'm bored with rice with sheep and goat fat."

Done deal. Once more, we would tempt fate, death. Nothing ventured, nothing gained: that was our philosophy, and we had nothing to lose. Except our lives.

We were off. When the younger boy brought us a bowl of food, Luca refused.

"We're not eating."

The boy was stunned. He looked at Luca, at a loss. He couldn't fathom why anyone wouldn't want to eat. For his people, food was a gift from heaven. He insisted, but Luca motioned for him to leave with the bowl. A few minutes later, Kindly appeared with the same bowl in his hands. He crouched down at the entrance to our shelter and handed us the food. Luca repeated that we would not eat, punctuating his words with a gesture of refusal, and he motioned to him to leave with the bowl. Kindly didn't understand why we didn't want to eat either. He frowned and turned on his heels.

In the following days, we repeated the same refusal at each meal. The boys left with the bowl of food, still unable to understand. We didn't live the same lives they did; their world was much harsher and crueler than ours. At the same time, we were valuable to them, and from their point of view it was probably a bad idea to let the hostages die of hunger.

After three or four days, Barbarossa had caught on. He came to bring us our bowl of food himself, along with Dentone and a Kalashnikov. Luca turned to me and looked me straight in the eye.

"Do not eat," he said firmly. "They're not going to shoot us, they're only going to threaten us. This is not the time to give up. Even if they point their guns at me, don't eat."

Luca had guessed Barbarossa's tactics perfectly. The old man knelt down and handed us the bowl.

"We're not eating," Luca said.

They took him outside and told him to go sit farther away. Barbarossa turned to me.

"*Madame, mangi.*"

He had a brutal look in his eyes, and a shiver ran down my spine. He held the bowl out to me insistently, but I refused. He sighed, and turned his gun on Luca.

"*Madame, mangi!*"

Luca was staring at me. I could see in his eyes that he was urging me not to touch the food. I turned to Barbarossa.

"Innocent," I said to him in my softest, calmest voice, "we are innocent."

I'm not sure, but I think he understood, because he lowered his gun. He and Dentone exchanged glances and he left.

From then on, the group tried everything to get us to eat, a new trick every day. They certainly didn't want to be forced to call their leader to tell him the Italian and the Canadian were starving to death. For two or three days, they ignored us, and didn't offer us anything to eat, trying to show us that they didn't care whether we ate or not. By the next day they were ready to shoot us if we didn't accept their food. Once, Barbarossa, looking demented, shoved a piece of sheep's liver at me with his knife. I watched the blood slide down the blade, along the handle and on Barbarossa's fingers, dripping onto the floor.

"*Madame, mangi!*"

I was still a vegetarian at that point, so his generous offer was that much less attractive. Another time, he took away our water. In Hassaniya, the Saharan dialect, the word for water is *il-me*.

"No *mangi*, no *il-me!*"

To get around the issue, Luca spoke to one of the young men, who hadn't been warned that we weren't supposed to drink until we agreed to eat, and the boy brought us water. Irate, Barbarossa scolded him, but we were allowed to keep the water.

Another day, Barbarossa threatened to separate Luca and me if I didn't eat. Then, to incite me to eat, he said immediately afterwards, "*Madame, mangi, madame* helicopter Canada."

I didn't flinch.

After about ten days, he took away our water again, and ordered the youngsters not to give us any. Running out of water in the intense heat of the desert isn't ideal, to say the least.

The next morning, Luca put his hand on my shoulder.

"Edith, listen. There's a new voice... It's not someone from the group."

He stood up to stick his head through the opening. I asked him what he could see.

"There's a man on a camel, sitting on a red saddle. In fact, it looks like a chair."

Who was he? We didn't get many visitors. Shortly afterwards, the stranger came and crouched down in front of the entrance to our lean-to with a can of condensed milk in his hand. Luca stood up as best he could, his head pushed up against the ceiling, and crouched down too. The man didn't seem to understand French; he was just holding out the milk can. Luca then showed him the empty water jug while pronouncing one of the first Hassaniya words we had learned: *il-me*. The man frowned and walked away with the jug. Luca almost smiled.

"I think we will have water."

The stranger returned with a gift from heaven—the jug filled to the brim with sweet, delicious water, the nectar of life. We had been deprived of water for more than twenty-four hours already, and we were beginning to be afraid. Once we had quenched our thirst, Luca gestured to ask the man what he wanted. The man handed him the can of condensed milk again.

"*Mangi!*"

Obviously, Barbarossa had taught him the word. Luca motioned to him that we weren't eating, so the man took a phone out of his pocket, and repeated his plea.

"*Mangi!*"

He explained to us, in gestures, that if we agreed to eat, we could make a video for our governments, proof that we were still alive, and that we would be released three days later. We were beginning to learn how to decipher the signs, gestures, and drawings in the sand.

After the man left, Luca turned to me.

"Lying is another one of their tactics."

We didn't believe him, and declined his offer. He shot his video anyway. It was nonsense: he filmed us watching him filming us. He then went back to the group, leaving the open milk can at the entrance of our shelter.

In the afternoon, Barbarossa left with the man. Three days later, he was back. As soon as he got off the camel, he came toward us with a letter in his hand. Luca took it, looked at it, and handed it to me to read. It was written in French, by a man who claimed to be the leader of the mujahideen who were holding us captive. Negotiations with Italy were non-existent for the moment, the letter said, so our hunger strike was doomed to failure, and it was better for us to start eating again. I folded the letter and gave it back to Barbarossa.

"*Mangi?*" he asked impatiently.

We shook our heads. "No *mangi.*"

One evening, Luca stepped outside to shake out our blanket full of sand, and I took the opportunity to go to the toilet. On my way back, I saw Barbarossa beating Luca with a stick, beating him back into the shelter. When the old man saw me, he looked at me and pointed inside the hideout place. He was angry, again. As a show of strength, the tyrant broke the stick in half over his knee, and then he whacked me in the back. We had to get into the shelter and not come out again; he had made his point. From that day on, Luca and I had to go to the toilet just outside the shelter, not too far away and without being seen.

On the eighteenth day of our fast, Barbarossa came to see us. I was lying on my side with my eyes closed.

"*Madame!*"

I ignored him. I didn't want to see his horrible face; I just wanted him to leave me alone.

"*MADAME!*" he cried.

I kept my eyes closed. I was sick of him. Luca later told me that he had seen fear in the old man's eyes. Barbarossa got up in a hurry and made a call, and less than an hour later a truck arrived. The three kids climbed in and left immediately. Only Barbarossa, Dentone, and Kindly remained. We were about to go, leaving the camels and the shelters behind.

Barbarossa motioned to us to climb into his truck. I had never seen him so angry; he was positively boiling. For once, his face was redder than his beard.

Nothing

AUGUST 26, 2019
252nd day in captivity

I sit, lie down.
I lie down, I sit up.
Eyes open, eyes closed—
Nothing.
Edith, are you sleeping?
I keep my eyes closed.
I'm waiting.

I open my eyes and sit up.
It's still too hot, I lie down again.
I close my eyes—
Nothing.
Not sleeping, waiting—

The ground beneath my feet buckles and fades
Into a maelstrom, my body falling,
Floating on dark shades
In the land of nothing.

I follow an old trail, blurred,
Wandering through an infinite hallway.
The lock clicks closed in every door.
My life is asleep. I've lost my way.

I brush aside the dark so I can see
And my fumbling feet trample the void,
But the darkness blooms exponentially
With roots I can't avoid.

[17]

The Fast,
Part Two

BARBAROSSA STOPPED THE truck. It was already dark, and there wasn't time to build a shelter, so we slept with the men under the vehicle. For the whole duration of the intensive aerial search, when there seemed to be millions of drones in the sky, the men would only move around on camels. They would fetch water from the well on camels, and bring back supplies—even sheep, tied up against the saddle. Barbarossa had agreed to take us in his truck that day only because he thought I was dying. When he finally saw that I wasn't, he was fuming. His emergency call had put many men on the move at a time when they should have stayed hidden.

The next morning, we settled down in the shade of the truck to protect ourselves from the sun. The desert was already warming; it was almost unimaginable that the night had been so cold. Luca saw that I was thirsty, and opened the door to grab our water. Big mistake! Dentone leapt toward the vehicle, gun in hand. Luca understood his error, but it was too late. He tried to explain, by pointing his finger at the water jug sitting in front of the passenger seat.

"*Il-me.*"

But Dentone refused to give it to him. Instead, he pointed to the sky.

"*Il-me, Italia!*"

Luca came back to me empty-handed.

"He talked about Italy... Do you think we're going home?"

"I don't know," Luca replied, shrugging his shoulders. "I hope so, because they've taken away our water again."

Right then, we heard the blathering of a camel in the distance. It's such a queer sound, like a wet cry. I can't explain it any other way: it sounds like the camels are screaming underwater. We had visitors once more.

The camel driver was a man in his thirties, fairly cheerful. He even came to greet us with a broad smile, which was rather unusual. The four men chatted for a good while around the fire. Later they got up and walked away to do who knows what. We couldn't see them anymore. Luca turned to me.

"Look, Edith, the canteen is hanging from the truck. Keep a look out while I go have a drink."

"Okay, but hurry. If they catch you, you're dead."

He rushed to the jug and drank a few sips of water.

"It's my turn to look out. Go drink, Edith."

I wasn't at all sure I wanted to risk it. I didn't move. Then a man came to get something from the truck, and left again immediately. Good thing I hadn't gone to get a drink; he would have caught me! But Luca insisted.

"Edith, go drink some water! We don't know when we'll have the chance again."

I made up my mind, and rushed to the canteen, but in my hurry I spilled all the water on myself and could only drink a few drops. I sat down next to Luca, my boubou soaking wet.

"Give me your jacket."

I was wearing a T-shirt underneath, so I took off my wet jacket, which might have given me away, and passed it to Luca.

"I didn't manage to drink anything."

"Shh, the men are coming back, be quiet."

The smiling man motioned that we should follow him. He led us to our new home. It was peculiar; the shelter had been dug out of the sand. I frowned: it looked like a grave. I pointed this out to Luca, who reassured me.

"It's probably to keep us hidden, and the ground will keep us cool on hot days."

Luca was right, it was a bit cooler underground, but they hadn't thought about the ants. We were attacked all day long. There must have been an anthill nearby, and ants bite hard! At night, mice scurried over us. I remember one night in particular, we were sleeping peacefully when a mouse jumped on Luca's face. He woke up with a start and threw the mouse into the air. The poor thing landed on my legs and I tossed it. It fell back on Luca, who immediately chased it away. The mouse was a ping-pong ball! Fortunately, it finally ran away.

The day after our first night in the dugout, an unknown camel driver came to pick up Barbarossa. We still had no water, and we were so thirsty. Kindly came to check that we were still alive in our hole.

"*Il-me?*" Luca asked.

But Kindly motioned that no, there was no more water for us.

"*Il-me, Italia,*" he added, pointing to the sky.

Another thing had changed: he no longer asked us whether we wanted to eat or not. At least we were left alone about that.

The day passed slowly. I was thirsty.

The next day was our second day without drinking, and the twenty-second without eating.

"Could you ask them for water? Tell them that I'm not well, that *Madame* is feeling bad."

Luca looked into my eyes.

"You want me to ask them for water? I already know the answer, but for you, I'll try anyway," he said, and climbed out of our hole.

He returned with Dentone escorting him, rifle in hand.

"What happened?"

"I tried everything, I even got down on my knees—you can imagine what it cost me to do that. They told me to leave, but I didn't move. Dentone threw embers at me to get me to leave, but I still didn't move. Then he grabbed his gun and here I am."

"Thank you, Luca, it's sweet of you to have tried so hard. They're real jerks. And we are in deep shit."

I went back to bed. It was a little windy and I concentrated on the wind brushing against my lips. It kept me from thinking too much about how thirsty I was. The day passed even more slowly than the previous one.

On the third day without water, Luca handed me a zipper he'd torn off a piece of clothing.

"Here, put this in your mouth, the metal will make you salivate a little."

I did what he asked, and he was right, it did make me drool.

On our fourth day without water, Luca had an idea.

"I'm going to drink my urine!"

"What?!" I stared at him quizzically.

"I need to pee. I'm going to drink my urine."

"Okay. Tell me what it's like."

He got up. A few seconds passed. I stood there smiling stupidly, thinking that Luca was drinking his pee.

He came back as if nothing had happened.

"So?"

"It's disgusting. It tastes strong. I didn't expect that. I didn't manage to drink it all, and now I have piss breath and a piss taste in my mouth."

I giggled. He made me laugh, my husband.

"Are you going to drink yours too?"

"No, not right now," I replied, laughing.

Our dugout in the ground was lined with long, slightly greasy grass. I took a blade—it was bright green.

"Have you ever noticed if camels eat this?" I asked Luca.

He thought for a moment.

"Yes, I think I've seen them eating it."

"If the camels eat the grass, it shouldn't be toxic for us, right?"

I put the fattest tip in my mouth and sucked at it. The grass contained a tiny bit of sweet juice, and I told Luca to take some too. He chose a good one and sucked the juice from it, then he got up and went outside to pick some more. I was ecstatic: sweet salvation!

Our fifth day without water, the twenty-fifth without food.

Again, a camel came blathering up. Luca peeked out of the hole. Barbarossa was back.

"*Il-me?*"

The old man seemed happy; he must have gotten some good news. He went to fill our water jug and handed it to Luca, as if nothing had ever happened. Luca handed me the jug and I hurried to drink. They both motioned to me to take it easy, and I tried to hold back, but I gulped at the water, divine water, sweet and pure water that... tasted like fuel. We were getting used to the tangy taste; the men used the same hose to fill the fuel tanks and the water jugs.

All the same, what a delight. I handed the jug to Luca so he could quench his thirst. As for Barbarossa, he went back to the men, happy, satisfied at something we didn't know.

[18]

Eyeglasses

THE NIGHT AFTER Barbarossa came back was terrible. My kidneys hurt like hell. My lower back seemed to be burning from the inside. I couldn't get comfortable. The pain was radiating everywhere, and there was nothing I could do.

The next morning, I explained to Luca how much pain I was in. He would have liked to help me, but there wasn't much he could do. When he touched my forehead he seemed worried: I was burning up. He told me to drink water, and I obeyed. He must have been right, it must have been the dehydration that was causing my suffering. Toward the end of the day my pain had subsided somewhat.

Suddenly, there was the sound of an engine in the distance. More visitors? There had been a lot of activity since our urgent move. It was already dark when Barbarossa came to the edge of our hole with a new stranger. He directed his flashlight straight at my face and I winced. Barbarossa pointed at me.

"*Madame!*"

I think he wanted the other man to see me. They left right away. I must not have looked so good, judging by the two big dark circles under Luca's eyes. The loss of muscle mass had turned him into a skeleton, and the same was probably true for me. I could see my bones, and my skin was desiccated. I was a shadow of my former self.

The next day I told Luca that I was thinking about starting to eat again. The lack of water had wiped us out, and I didn't hold out much hope of surviving if we didn't eat soon. Luca had been worried about me the day before, and he agreed.

"Go and ask for milk," I suggested. "Tell them that *Madame* is not well."

Luca did, returning with the stranger who'd arrived the day before. The man leaned over our hole, and asked me what was going on. The visitor spoke French—a miracle! He looked like an important man, outranking our guards. He was well dressed, and wore glasses, so we named him Eyeglasses.

Luca explained to him that we hadn't eaten for twenty-five days and that I wasn't feeling well. The man told us to be patient, he had to go make a phone call. I was relieved. He seemed nice, our Eyeglasses—I mean, compared to the others. Shortly afterwards he came back with a glass of milk, and told us to sip it slowly. He hadn't been able to find condensed or powdered milk, so he gave us camel milk. Camel milk is extremely nutritious, and given our long fast, we had to sip it slowly. As we drank, the man explained that he had come to shoot a video of us, which he would pass on to our families. He suggested we bathe first.

"We have no soap," Luca said.

"Don't you?" The man was surprised. "I'll be right back."

We hadn't washed for six weeks, since the flight into the desert. I was happy to finally be able to clean myself a little. It's crazy how such mundane things take on a whole new meaning when we feel their absence.

So we shot a short video for our families—proof of life, though I learned later, once I got out of that nightmare, that my family had never received it. Eyeglasses set off again on his camel, with some others. Then a man arrived on a motorbike, delivered a message to the guards, and disappeared. That same evening, another new vehicle appeared. There were lots of comings and goings. Something was brewing but, as usual, we didn't understand.

The next morning, Dentone brought us a piece of bread for breakfast and then, around ten o'clock, Barbarossa appeared in front of our shelter.

"*Madame!*" he bellowed, pointing at my shoes and my blanket.

Luca immediately stiffened up, worried that Barbarossa would want to take off with me again.

"What's going on?" he asked. "I don't like this. Where is *Madame* going?"

"*Madame* Canada," the old man replied, pointing to the sky.

What? I was going to Canada? What about Luca? I stared at Barbarossa.

"And *Monsieur*?" I asked.

Luca would be leaving later, he explained.

"One month, two months, three months, *Monsieur* Italy."

We were stunned. We didn't move; we didn't know how to react. Barbarossa showed me the truck parked a little ways away. I motioned to him to wait, and I turned to Luca. My eyes filled with tears.

"I can't leave you here alone."

"Don't worry, Canada just worked faster than Italy."

I huddled in his arms. I can't describe the sadness I felt. He was so small, so frail, so different from the athletic, energetic Luca of before. I would be leaving behind the ghost of the man I had known. But I knew that I couldn't argue with our kidnappers, that I had to leave Luca, abandon him to his fate. My belly was in knots and my sadness flowed and overflowed.

Barbarossa had had enough. He motioned for me to take my blanket and follow him to the truck. But I couldn't even manage to carry the blanket: I had grown so weak that it was too heavy for me, and the driver had to carry it to the vehicle. I didn't dare to turn back to Luca; I was too torn. I would have liked to fight, but I knew how these men operated; I knew it wouldn't get me anywhere.

As we were leaving the camp, I mustered the courage to take one last look at Luca. This brave man had taken care of me as best he could; he had fought for me. Now, motionless, he watched me leave. I tried to hold back my tears; I didn't want to show the driver the depth of my despair.

It was March 4, 2019, the seventy-seventh day of our captivity. A dark day.

Torn

MARCH 25, 2019
98th day in captivity

A tremor furrowed the earth anew,
Tearing the ground on its way
And swallowing up the reckless few
Who dared cross it on their journey.

On the other shore I held out my hands
But my fingers lost his, receding...
The rift between us opened without
   a single sound
That might have offered warning.

I shouted, I wanted the world to stand still
But my cry echoed out and waned,
An endless ricochet in the dim
Place where souls are forsaken.

PART V

The Women

Daughter of the Dunes

MARCH 22, 2019
95th day in captivity

In the long shadow of the night,
Lost in thoughts faraway,
Beneath the stars' infinite light
The woman of sunny dunes lay.

A star burst into a thousand sparks
Rippling out, the pulse of the earth
In its deep, parched heart
Raining down on this daughter of the desert.

Then life began in the earth's fertile belly,
In a great oasis it spread
And the lady blinked beautifully
And breathed the serpentine heat.

Light flashed, flickered, and shone
On beating wings: the gossamer slip
Of a dragonfly wandering alone
Through its dappled oasis.

From the top of its perch, the sun
Danced with the woman, beyond age.
But the desert alone
Remembered her birth within a mirage.

19

The White Tent

WE TRAVELED ACROSS the dunes for around sixty miles. The landscape unfurled blue and yellow before my eyes, repeating itself endlessly, but I hardly paid attention. Nor was I much concerned with how this sand cowboy drove.

I kept thinking of how I could get Luca out of this ordeal, but nothing I came up with seemed any good. The thought of being separated from Luca, unable to help him, was devastating. It made me sick. Barbarossa had told us that in two or three months Luca would be able to return to Italy, and I held on to that hope, but I didn't quite believe it. I could hardly believe I was on my way to Canada. They'd already lied to us more than once.

The young driver seemed to be looking for something, and I snapped back to the real world. There was another man, also fairly young, in the back of the truck. He was the digger: his job was to clear the truck when it got stuck in the sand. It was the first time I had traveled with only two men. Usually they moved in groups of six. We stopped near a well, and the driver got out and walked around it, peering at the dunes. He seemed to be searching for tracks. When he didn't find what he was looking for, he sat back down at the wheel and we drove to another dune. This time it was the digger who got off. He left on foot, and I lost sight of him. He came back after about twenty minutes, having found nothing. We continued on our way. From time to time the digger would bang on the cab window to signal to the driver, I had no idea what about.

Later on we stopped again. The driver got out of the pickup and fired about thirty shots in the air, emptying both Kalashnikovs. It was bizarre and, as usual, I didn't understand. Shortly afterwards, in lieu of lunch, I sipped the milk the driver had prepared for me. The driver scanned the horizon with his binoculars.

We set off, and drove for half an hour before arriving at a camp. Six men gathered around a fire waved at us. The driver laid my blanket under a tree a few yards away, and told me to sit down and stay there. I waited under that tree for an hour before two unknown men with turbans appeared. They gestured at me to get up and follow them, and I did, but with difficulty. I was dizzy and I still had a hard time dragging my blanket around. The heat was too intense for my tired body.

We climbed a small dune, and at the bottom of the other side stood a white tent. The men escorted me to the mysterious shelter. Inside I saw two women, sitting, staring at me. Were they desert women? The men's wives?

One of them seemed to be in shock, staring into space. As for the other, I had the feeling she was a healer. Maybe our captors wanted to fix me up a bit before sending me back to Canada. Both women had dark skin, burned by the desert sun. As I watched them, I heard the voice of another woman behind me. She had come from a shelter hidden under the branches of an acacia tree. She spoke Tamasheq, the language of the Tuareg, and chatted with the two men escorting me. The desert Arabs seemed to have a rudimentary grasp of Tamasheq, though they often spoke Hassaniya or Arabic. After some discussion, the two turbaned men left, and the woman returned to her shelter to get shampoo, soap, a toothbrush, and a tin of sardines.

"Here," she said, "*c'est pour toi*. You can go into the tent with the other two women."

How about that. The woman who spoke Tamasheq spoke French, too.

"You speak French very well," I said, surprised.

"Come inside, it's hot. The men will bring you water so you can wash yourself."

I thanked the woman, who was already walking away to her acacia tree. I later learned that she had been separated from the other two women because of frequent conflicts between them.

I turned to the healer and smiled.

"*Bonjour!*" She smiled back.

"You speak French too?" I exclaimed.

"So does she." She indicated the other woman, the one who was staring out into space. "When we are together, we speak French."

So they weren't desert women.

"Who are you?"

The healer looked at me for a long time.

"We are hostages. The woman who lives under the acacia tree has been held captive in the desert for three years. I've been here for two and a half years, and the nun, two years.

Two years? Three years? I couldn't believe it.

"And who are you?" she asked.

"I've been held for three months, but they told me I was getting out today."

I was floored, because I was starting to understand.

"I'm sorry, but I don't think you're leaving the desert just yet," she said kindly.

She looked at me with sad eyes, then dropped her gaze to the shampoo, soap, toothbrush, and sardines I was holding. I heard the truck drive off, leaving for good. The truth hit me, and it hurt. Everything seemed to suggest that I had been dropped off here to stay for a long time. Two years, three years... It had only been three months for me.

The healer told me her story. I had never seen such sad eyes in my life. Her tale was one of the most heartbreaking and poignant, but also one of the most frustrating I'd ever heard. It brought tears to my eyes, and broke my heart to pieces.

For confidentiality, I will withhold the real names of these beautiful women. I will call the healer Elisabeth. The woman with the blank stare I will call Linda, which means beautiful in Spanish, and the lady in the tree, Mirage.

When she had finished speaking, Elisabeth turned to Linda.

"You too, tell her your story."

But Linda's eyes were dull. She didn't answer, didn't move. Elisabeth explained that Linda was unsettled because she hadn't been expecting a new guest, and so it was Elisabeth who told me her story too. What a nightmare! Those two women had dedicated their lives to saving people, and now they were being held hostage. The injustice shocked and outraged me deeply.

That night I couldn't sleep, I felt like I was floating, as if my feet were no longer touching the ground and my head was drifting randomly through space, totally detached from reality. I felt that way for a week.

20

Poetry

DURING THEIR LONG captivity, the women had acquired some useful items—nail clippers, a sewing needle, a pocket mirror, a toothbrush, a teapot.

Linda lent me her mirror so I could clean my face. I hadn't properly washed in over a month. It was pretty horrible. I still remember the shock of seeing my face. I was beastly! My skin was more wrinkled than an old woman's, likely from dehydration. I had dark circles around my eyes—grayish, almost black. My bones were poking through my skin, and I was skeletal. This wasn't a woman's face, and certainly not my own, just some poor ragged creature's. Would I ever get my old face back, smooth and rosy, or would I forever be scarred by my ordeal? *I don't look like this in real life,* I wanted to tell the women, but I think they knew. They probably already understood my pain, just as I could see theirs in every glance.

Yet amid the affliction there were beautiful moments, too, mercifully. Elisabeth had a notebook and a pen, objects that, to my eyes, came straight from heaven. How much faster time would pass if I could write poems! We always managed to find bits of cardboard in the women's camp, especially when we received food or boxes of tea. All I needed was a pen, and there it was, right next to Elisabeth. On March 19, 2019, two weeks after I'd arrived, I finally dared to ask her.

"Do you think I could borrow your pen to write a poem?"

"Of course!" Elisabeth replied, happy to make me happy.

And she handed me her treasure. I was eager to show my gratitude and asked her to tell me the first word that came to her mind.

"Well, I love light," she said. "That's your word, light."

Great, she was willing to play along. I could write her a poem. I loved Elisabeth, a wonderful woman with a big heart. She was suffering a great deal: she had a tumor the size of a cantaloupe in her right breast, and she was weak from malnutrition and physical inactivity. She was over seventy years old, and lived in unimaginable conditions. From time to time, a man came to the camp and deigned to give her some medicine. He claimed to be a doctor, but wasn't, according to Elisabeth. The man had once stepped on a mine, she told me, which explained his prosthetic leg.

Mirage and Linda were suffering, too, but psychologically: they heard voices. I know that in Linda's case, it was due to the trauma of being kidnapped by the small-time bandits who handed her over to Nusrat al-Islam, which was the Saharan branch of Al-Qaeda that was responsible for our forced detention. On the day of the kidnapping, the assailants had entered the orphanage where Linda had been working and demanded money. Alas, the nuns had nothing to give them, and their meager possessions were deemed insufficient. Linda begged the men to leave the other women alone: if they were to hurt anyone, she asked them to take her, the oldest of the four. With a wave of their Kalashnikovs, they motioned that she should follow them, and they set off on their motorbikes toward the north. They rode for five or six days, until Linda and Elisabeth were brought together. The shock, the exhaustion, and the terror had wreaked havoc on her mental state.

The voice Linda heard in her head was that of an old man, who tormented her day and night. He said such terrible things that she sometimes cried out in despair, or felt nauseated. Sometimes, this gentle, submissive woman yelled back against the voice to silence it; she seemed to be speaking to no one. How could we help her? I once tried to explain to her that the hallucination was causing her suffering, but she couldn't seem to understand. She insisted that the voice was real; she could hear it in her ears. She thought it was one of the mujahideen harassing her because she didn't like the right god. He wanted her to convert to Islam, so he hurled accusations at her, sins real or invented, to unsettle her.

After I tried to reason with her, the torturous voice seemed to become more intense. I felt helpless, I didn't know how to help Linda out of her madness. Couldn't such a generous, gentle, fragile woman have a moment's peace? As if the endless days weren't enough, she slept badly, and her nights were endless, too. She was drawn and exhausted, though she had found some tricks to survive the psychological attacks of the old mujahideen. Sometimes she sang all day long to try to drown out the evil voice. It broke my heart that we had no way to help.

As for Mirage, she'd been alone for a year before the other two women arrived. Deprived of everything—human contact, joy, laughter, compassion, friendship—she had languished in isolation, sadness, and despair, crushed by constant threats, devastated by misunderstanding and fear. I know now that living in such conditions can make you quite ill. I don't know if Mirage was sick before she was taken, but when I met her she was no longer sane, and she had a way of upsetting others, especially her captors.

How could they treat them this way, women who had sacrificed their lives for the poor? No one deserves to suffer so much, and especially not in the name of Allah. These women were as religious as their captors, but their god had a different name, and the mujahideen therefore deemed them unworthy. The women would be condemned on the day of judgment, and so the men had no qualms about condemning them in advance on earth. Like messengers, draped in their truths and implacable morals, the mujahideen were giving these women a taste of hell.

Personally, I believe in Life, in a higher power, but not in religion or in the notion of divine judgment, which I consider arbitrary. As long as humans have existed, there have been gods, but they change, they multiply; sometimes they are forgotten, and sometimes they become part of history. They look like men or like animals, or sometimes they're half human and half animal. Where was paradise before the revelations of the Prophet? Was the garden empty? Was God impatiently waiting for the right religion to be founded before deciding to occupy heaven? I've always preferred to believe in Life rather than thinking that I was born into the right religion, or on the right continent or in the right country, or with the right skin color. There is beauty in diversity, and religion is simply part of the culture of a people. It can even be beautiful if it isn't used to justify violence.

"Lady Light" is the title of the first poem I wrote in captivity. I dedicated it to my Lady Light, Elisabeth. When I read it to her, she was elated.

"Wow! This is great! You have talent. You should write a book of poetry while you're here with us. I'll lend you my pen, you can use it whenever you want."

Elisabeth was so encouraging. She liked to say that in every misfortune, a door can open. Her kindness showed me my own door, the gift that would allow me to fly away, to let my soul out of the cage where time dragged on.

I listened to Elisabeth, and wrote almost a poem a day, though I couldn't keep them all.

When I was finally free, I had managed to take fifty-seven poems with me. I carried them in a bag hidden at my waist, under my clothes, at the risk of losing them if my kidnappers caught me.

Fifty-seven poems and a jug of water.

Lady Light

MARCH 19, 2019
92nd day in captivity

Light weaves over the water,
Trailing its tattered train,
Its ancestral specter.
On the river it ripples and wanes.

The gaze falters, shimmering
And shatters into a rain of slivers
Over the insatiable river, leaving
A face etched on the water.

A hand dips into the light,
A woman quenches her thirst
For life—a whole river's might
Flows through the brittle desert.

21

Five Months

I LIVED WITH THE women from March 4 to August 15, 2019, in four separate camps.

May is the hottest month of the year there; temperatures can soar to 120°F in the shade. Our daily water rations were clearly insufficient. I would have liked to drink more—my body demanded it—but we had to restrain ourselves. The wells were often far from the camps, and they tended to dry up during the hot season. By "camp," I mean an area that included at least two acacia trees hidden by the dunes. That was where we would set up and take down our tents. Our drivers would choose our new temporary home by driving around the desert. We had to be on the move all the time, and never leave a trace.

I learned to cook with what we had. For example, I made a kind of rustic cheese during the dry season. I dissolved powdered milk in water with a little salt, and put the pot in the sun. Two days later we had cheese. All that was left was to let it drain through a cloth. That was the Tuareg method of cheesemaking. It's as easy as that in the desert.

In the desert, people bake bread in the sand, and I'd learned how by watching Barbarossa. You dig a hole, light a fire, and wait for coals to form. The coals are removed and a flatbread is placed in the bottom of the hole, on the black, burning sand. The bread is sprinkled with light-colored sand to protect it from the burning coals, which are then placed back on top, before the whole thing is covered with sand. A hole in the sand becomes a small oven, and all you have to do is wait for your bread à l'étouffée! Once the bread is cooked, you dig it up and smack it to remove the sand that's stuck to it.

We didn't have many ingredients, but I'm a cook by trade, and with a bit of imagination I was able to diversify our meals. It kept me busy, and the women were happy, because they used to eat only rice or pasta with oil or tomato paste.

Linda liked to keep busy with embroidery. Over the course of months, she and Mirage had collected pieces of old tarpaulins that had been used as tents, and had salvaged white threads from the weave of the tarps and a few colored threads from scarves or scraps of fabric.

One day Linda gave me a bag she had embroidered, decorated with pretty flowers. I loved my little purse, which I used to hold my soap, shampoo, and my toothbrush—that wonderful thing. I had gone three months without brushing my teeth, and I didn't yet know the African method of chewing acacia stems and roots to clean my teeth.

Linda had also generously given me one of her blankets, so I wouldn't be so cold at night, a pair of socks, and a traditional garment worn by men in the desert. If she'd had more, she would have given me more. I was in the company of extraordinary women— genuinely generous, humane, compassionate. They were willing to heal any wound, to help anyone regardless of their religion, their beliefs, the color of their skin. They had saved hundreds of orphans who otherwise wouldn't have survived the harshness of life in Mali.

Elisabeth told me that she had once rescued an infant from a trash heap. She had brought babies home to watch over them overnight after finding them in critical condition. As soon as they were safe, she took them back to the orphanage. The women gave selflessly. The fate of hostages was also incredibly difficult, but they sacrificed what they could to help others. I loved them so much. My heart breaks when I think of them, still trapped in the desert. Every day I hope for news that they've been released. I remember my dear friends every day, and just thinking about their suffering takes my breath away.

I wanted to give them a gift too, and one day I realized that I had something priceless with me. I've always loved having baubles in my hair, and the year before I had wrapped some of my dreadlocks in pretty threads. I had a paradise of bright colors in my hair! I told Linda she could unravel the threads from my dreadlocks and use them in her embroidery. That woman with a heart of gold shared scraps of fabric and let me use her needle, and we took turns decorating our bags with vivid colors—red, orange, yellow, blue, and purple; we had the whole rainbow.

We were far from being the only inhabitants of the desert: there were also flies. This was no offhand observation. There was an infinite number of flies, and they seemed to go completely nuts when they saw any living being. They rushed into our nostrils, our eyes, our mouths, and our ears, attracted by mucous membranes. How can I even explain? One morning, very early, when I came back from going to the toilet, I heard Elisabeth muttering.

"One hundred and forty-eight! At one-fifty, I stop counting."

"What exactly are you counting?"

"How many flies I've killed."

Two things are true: we had nothing to do, and there were far too many flies.

The desert is not a particularly peaceful place. We were attacked by demented insects every second, relentlessly, all day long. The lizards took advantage of the mass killings, as Linda and Elisabeth were quick to feed them dead flies. Our desert also had scorpions and vipers. I never had a run-in with those critters personally, but since I couldn't see much without my contact lenses, I may have brushed past a few without realizing it.

In the morning, we often found snake tracks around the tent, but there were never any incidents. Elisabeth did wake up one day with a scorpion in her pants, and another time with a snake coiled by her head, but she was more frightened than hurt. The only ones who suffered were those poor creatures, who were killed by the men when Mirage alerted them to their presence.

There were birds in the desert too. One particularly hot afternoon, a young bird, no doubt seeking protection from the heat, came into the tent and hid behind my bag of blankets. I'd noticed that birds had a hard time surviving in the desert during the dry season. Elisabeth poured some water into a tin and placed it next to my bag.

"She's pretty, we could call her Nuage," I said, putting down my embroidery.

I watched as the bird came out of hiding to get a drink of water. The women nodded in agreement. Nuage—cloud—was a perfect name.

Cloud came and went throughout the day, and my bag became her little home. A few days later, she brought two of her sisters with her. One of them hid behind Linda's bag, and the other one made her home with Elisabeth. Each of us three took care of a bird. We gave them bread to eat and fresh water to drink.

The fledglings grew quickly. Each one had her own character: mine was the boldest, Elisabeth's was the most delicate and discreet, and Linda's had a highly developed territorial instinct. They would come eat out of our hands, and land on our heads, shoulders, feet, or arms, waiting for us to feed them. They made our days pass a little more quickly. Alas, one day, we had to move camp, and that magical kinship came to an end.

Like the desert, our life as captives was ninety-nine percent desolation and one percent abundance. Just enough to get us through another day.

Secret Garden

Lost in light
The darkness cannot reach.
A small patch, out of sight
Burns the shadows with its touch.

Everywhere shades flicker and lurk,
Snuffling at the edge of virtue.
A sweet scent reminds the dark
Of the evening it first passed through.

Life has a secret garden
Embraced in its luminous veins.
Its heart beats, unconcerned
And on the resplendent earth exhales again.

In the garden where twined trees bloom,
Rooted in ancient sibylline mists,
Nature sheds itself like brume
As the glinting lush of chimeras persists.

The moon and sun are one and the same.
Sharing the same sphere
They fade, blaze, and flame
Like jewels in the air.

A river snakes across the grove,
Weaving a pulsing core.
Its current holds a treasure trove
That feeds and quenches the shore.

Only souls forever in passing
May cross into this sanctuary.
The door is open, the garden an offering—
Rest on the flight to infinity.

[22]

Storms in
the Sahara

I N THE AREA where the women's camps were, the rainy season
lasted from mid-July to mid-September. We weren't in the
most remote part of the desert, where nothing survives. There
were occasional acacia trees, a few bushes, tufts of tall grasses
growing through the sand. There was nothing gentle: the plants
were thorny, the heat was suffocating, the spiders and scorpions
were poisonous, and the flies were insane. The men carried weapons and the storms were preternaturally fierce.

When the rainy season came, the nights were still hot, so the
air seemed even heavier and more humid. It was so warm in the
tent that we always slept outside. Elisabeth told me that the rains
would start around July 15. I guess Mother Nature was eager to
show me what she could do, because the first rain showers came
early.

On July 9, 2019, the day was unbearably hot and humid. Elisabeth gazed into the distance; the clouds were black, and lightning
streaked the sky. A storm rumbled a few miles away and seemed to
be coming toward us.

"Maybe it will change course and blow out to sea," Elisabeth said.

"It might be best if we sleep in the tent tonight," Linda added;
she was also used to desert storms. We wouldn't have much time

to shelter when the storm came, she explained to me. Perhaps it would be better to get into the tent immediately, tie down our belongings, and secure the tarp in the sand.

"No," Elisabeth said. "I think the storm will turn, the winds are changing."

She suggested that we put our things in the tent as a precaution, but sleep outside anyway. It was so hot that being confined inside was a last resort, and only to protect us during the storm, if it did hit.

Soon the sky was roaring like a lion leaping upon its prey. Ominous black clouds churned and lightning slashed across the sky. The roiling shadows were moving quickly toward our camp. Farther away, the men were also hiding their stuff under a tarp. There was nothing we could do but wait and hope. On that grand, theatrical stage where the night waltzed with the elements, I fell asleep. It was magnificent.

A harsh, coarse wind woke me in the middle of the night. Already I was covered in sand. In the blinding gusts I began to search for my two friends. The sand was everywhere and it hurt my eyes, but I finally saw Elisabeth and Linda struggling in the wind to get their blankets into the tent. We had to be quick; the rain could start any second. The wind had already blown away some of our precious goods, and the sand had buried much of what we'd tucked under the tarp.

"Close up all the openings!" Linda shouted at me.

I tried to do as she asked, but the wind fought me, pulling at the tarp. In the end the god of wind got the better of us, and we didn't manage to seal the tent. It began to pour, and we huddled in the center of the tent, but the tarp was torn and water gushed down on us and our belongings. We had to hold on.

An hour later, the rain had moved on to moisten the desert elsewhere, leaving us battered and wet. I asked the others if they were all right; they didn't answer, but their tense expressions spoke volumes. All our blankets were soaked, and the wind was still blowing fiercely. To think that we had been so hot just a few hours before, and now we were shivering under our wet blankets. That was how we spent the night, trying to sleep in spite of the cold.

The next morning, when I awoke, Linda was already busy straightening the pieces of wood that had collapsed on us during the night. I got up to give her a hand raising the tent. Once it was more or less back up, we walked around the camp to assess the damage.

As we were laying our blankets out to dry, I saw that our fire-wood was soaked too. I took it upon myself to go ask the men for some gasoline to light a fire, which would be more than welcome. To go see the men, we had to cross the small dune that separated us from them. As their religion dictated, men and women could not share the same space.

That was my introduction to the fury of storms in the Sahara.

The Storm

JULY 9, 2019
204th day in captivity

The shadows crawled and creaked,
Slipped into cracks in the ground.
The clouds were charged, electric
And light snapped and billowed around.

Nature took a plunging bow:
The sky churned by in a trance,
The wind bending low
As it coursed over flying sand.

The lightning seized the moment—
White canvas thrashed and torn.
Clouds pealed above the howling tent
Where three women cowered in the storm.

The sky moved along its baleful way
And everywhere shattered the drought.
The storm swirled and swayed,
Easily heaving the desert's weight.

Static rippled across the firmament
Ripping each beast from its lair
And the storm gathered its thunder and went
Leaving the women, the gale in their hair.

PART VI

The Migration

CAPTIVITY: DAY 241 TO DAY 243

The Edge of the World

Whoever said the earth was round
Didn't see this edge, my feet
Swinging out into space—I found
The brink, where world and nothing meet.

I want to rest but wait, restless.
Time stretches and doubles back
As I sit here—where the wind ceases,
Where blue dwindles into black.

The void lifts up to graze my limbs
And forever burrows in my palm:
This is where the sun begins
To birth its colors, shining on.

I wait and watch a tumbling brook
Falling and falling into the abyss,
But the world shines back, and already it looks
Like a mirror's infinite kiss.

Gravity holds me by a crystal thread,
My own hue runs a deep blue steel.
I watch and wait, I turn to lead.
The unknown, the void is at my heels.

[23]

The Hunt

ELISABETH STRAIGHTENED UP.

"Put on your scarf," she said, "there's a man coming."

All three of us covered our hair and necks. The man stopped at the entrance to our tent and spoke with Elisabeth. The men always addressed her because she was the oldest woman in our group.

With signs and gestures, the visitor conveyed that I was to take my blanket and my bag, because I was leaving. I was in shock. Leaving, again? Now I was going to be separated from the women? Elisabeth turned to me and told me that I had to pack up.

"Maybe you're going to get out," she said.

I didn't believe it. I had already been fooled once, and I wasn't going to make the same mistake again. As Elisabeth explained what I had already understood, the man waited patiently. I packed my things and hugged the women goodbye one last time.

It was early afternoon on August 15 when I got into a new truck that had arrived that morning. I didn't know why I was leaving. My only hope was finding Luca, but I knew there wasn't much chance of that.

I recognized the young driver: he was the one who had brought me to the women's camp five months earlier. I had to hold on tight, because we would ride across the desert like we were running a rodeo on the dunes. He was foolhardy, so I decided to name him Hardy. But I was stronger now, I could withstand the thumps and jolts and not get tossed around so much, like last time.

The team that was leaving with me was new. Apart from the driver and me in the cab, there were three fighters I didn't know in the back, sitting on a pile of travel gear and accessories, water, and diesel, all tied down with a net. We headed north, Hardy driving like a madman through the dunes, slaloming between mounds of sand and clumps of tall grass. I have to admit he was a good driver... although he had placed a hand grenade on the dash, and it rolled around all over the place, smacking into the panel at every bump and turn.

All of a sudden, the men behind us started to get agitated, banging on the steel wall of the cab, presumably trying to tell the driver something. I squinted to see if there was any unusual movement in the distance, but it was all a blur. Hardy slammed his foot down on the gas; we were driving dangerously fast now, zigzagging between obstacles.

A gazelle? Was that a gazelle I saw running ahead of us? I couldn't believe it, but Hardy was on the hunt. The poor animal tried to escape, but our machine was tireless, and we pursued it relentlessly. The gazelle leapt, changed direction abruptly, and spun to run back in the opposite direction, but Hardy refused to give up. I kept looking from the grenade to the gazelle, and from the gazelle to the grenade. The men in the back weren't firing, and I realized that the tactic was to wear the animal down, when suddenly a tire burst and Hardy had to stop. The men looked disappointed.

But—a twist of fate!—once they'd changed the tire, the gazelle reappeared and the chase picked up again. The poor thing had really thrown itself into the lion's den. We drove behind the animal, honking our horn like mad. How scared it must have been. Half an hour later, it finally collapsed from exhaustion. The gazelle had given everything it had to survive.

Hardy pulled a small blade from a trunk, got out of the truck, and slowly approached the gazelle. It didn't even try to get up. I think it knew its life was over. Hardy slit the animal's throat and bled it, then stowed his trophy in the back with the three men.

The hunt was over, and we continued north.

[24]

Racing North

NIGHT FELL, PAINTING the world in darkness, and the moon rose, full and bright. The conditions were right to let us drive with our lights off after sunset. My driver was obviously keen to keep a low profile.

The wind picked up; a storm was approaching and was already shaking the sky above us. We reached a well, where Hardy busied himself drawing a large circle in the sand, going around in circles with the truck. Was that how the men communicated with each other in the desert? I had the distinct impression that we were looking for another group. A man fired a rifle into the sky, and we all listened for an answer that didn't come.

Were we late because of the gazelle hunt? Had we missed a meeting? Hardy told me to get out of the truck. The wind was blowing hard, and thunder roared in the distance; the storm was stalking us. Hardy prepared a bowl of milk for me. There was meat in the truck, the gazelle, but I had the feeling that it was meant to be shared with those we should have been meeting that night.

I tried to drink the milk, but it was full of sand. It's hard to eat or drink when the wind picks up in the desert. It started to rain, and great gusts of wind tore at my clothes. Hardy motioned for me to get back into the pickup with him and another of the men. We were cramped on the front seat, and the prescribed distance between the men and me, a woman, could not be respected. The other two sat in the back of the pickup, protecting themselves as best they could from the weather.

We slept for a while, until the rain stopped battering the truck. The wind was still blowing wildly, whistling and carrying the whole landscape with it in its frantic rush. Hardy cleared his throat to get my attention, then waved me off to sleep outside. I wasn't sad to leave the small, cramped cabin, and I lay down on the sand, swaddled in my blanket. Sleeping in the maelstrom of a sandy wind is an interesting experience, to say the least.

In the morning we got up early to resume our search. We hadn't driven far when two pickup trucks appeared. We stopped and got out of our vehicle, and the men greeted each other. They immediately lit a fire and began to carve up the gazelle. I sat a bit farther off, waiting patiently to see what would happen. They fed me well, and even gave me mango juice! I hadn't had fruit juice since I was captured; it was such a treat. The men also offered me tea. They were all kind to me, which was comforting: I had lost the habit of kindness and attention. The trip felt like a break for me, an in-between time, which gave me strength and courage to face the events to come.

After breakfast, Hardy motioned to me to get into another vehicle, and so I changed teams and drivers. I was relieved because these men were almost friendly. My new driver even greeted me in my own language.

"You speak French?" I asked, surprised.

"*Un peu*," he replied with a thick accent.

Un peu—any French!—was fine by me.

I was alone in the truck with him; the other men were traveling in the second vehicle. As for Hardy and his men, they went on their own way, and I never saw them again.

I called the new driver Mangusio, because he gave me so many bottles of mango juice that I wasn't even able to drink them all on

the trip. Put them in your bag for later, he told me. He motioned
that I should fasten my seatbelt, which surprised me; no one
before him seemed to care about my safety. But just my luck, the
belt was defective, and I had to do without. Within seconds, the
two trucks were speeding at 110 miles per hour. Now I understood
why Mangusio had asked me to buckle up! I took a deep breath.
Que sera, sera! Going 110 on the sand, over dunes and obstructions,
I wasn't sure we would survive.

I suspected we were trying to cross the northern border of Mali
into Algeria; otherwise why were we driving so fast? And why
were the men in the other truck armed to the teeth? For two days I
had been watching the direction of the sun and shadows, and had
deduced that we were heading northeast. My Algeria hypothesis
seemed credible. Perhaps we were crossing an area where there
was a higher risk of encountering enemies.

Still, I allowed myself some optimism. Maybe I was finally
going to get out of Africa. If not, why were they treating me as if
I had suddenly put my human skin back on? Why all the mango
juice? Elisabeth had once told me that she thought Tamanrasset,
in southern Algeria, was a possible way out. A mujahideen had
mentioned the town. Elisabeth herself had thought she was going
to go that way, at one point, but in the end, they had turned back
after several days of driving north. Something had changed, and
Elisabeth remained in the hands of her captors.

There was nothing going on that hinted that I was about to
be set free, but the trip did get my hopes up, perhaps despite my
better judgment. At the same time, I wanted to spare myself possible disappointment, but it was hard, it's so hard not to believe.
Life in captivity is so predetermined that every time something
out of the ordinary happens, the brain goes into overdrive. What
if today is the day? What if I get to see Luca again? What if we get
to go home together? It was painful to think about him, since I
didn't know where he was or how he was doing, or even if he was

still alive. He had probably tried to escape, knowing him, and who knows how that would have ended.

We flew over the sands of the Sahara at full speed for a good two hours, and I hoped that Mangusio wouldn't lose control of the truck. We were lucky that the road seemed clear now. The land-scape looked plain, empty of life, of anything remarkable. At one point we finally slowed down to a slightly more normal speed. The border or the danger zone must have been behind us.

It's hard to explain, but by that point in the whole calamitous situation, I felt numb, as if nothing could get a reaction out of me. At one point we almost plowed into the other men's truck, which had stopped. Mangusio, who had probably been distracted, jerked the steering wheel suddenly, narrowly avoiding an accident, and we slid up a dune before coming to a halt ourselves. I didn't bat an eye. I didn't give a shit about anything. I felt amorphous, inert; an empty shell. The men told me what to do and I obeyed. I had noth-ing to say; my life no longer belonged to me. I no longer had the strength to fight against oblivion. I had become docile, a puppet in their hands.

I was their hostage: both a treasure and a nobody.

End of the World

SEPTEMBER 24, 2019
281st day in captivity

I wade through time: it marches on.
I wander the world as it ends,
Wondering where sensation has gone
And who remembers passion's last stand.

This is how it ends:
A crooked, misshapen world.
Still I search, heart in hand
Even if only for the same old . . .

You know I'm a wanderer.
I don't know what to do.
I walk backwards, I waver—
Yet I must see myself through.

The world is of stone
And I sink in the scree.
In cities made of concrete and bone
The people sleep in the streets.

I stumble alone through back alleys,
Slump in dumpsters' dull steel.
There's no blue sky, no green valley.
Everything so fake it almost seems unreal.

continued overleaf

And you: what will you do?
You see only torment, only loss.
Fear walks behind you
Bringing nothing but chaos.

Take my hand: I am with you—
Do you see the world fade away?
We will search through the refuse
For mystical light, another day.

Tell me: are you dying?
I can't see you clearly anymore.
There are only your memories, failing...
Have we found the end, the other shore?

25

Sandstorm

THERE WAS SOMETHING odd in the distance, like a wall stretching from the ground to the sky. Mangusio motioned to me to roll up my window. Was it a sandstorm? I couldn't see very well. Suddenly the truck in front of us disappeared, and the sight made every hair on my body stand on end. All at once I was no longer resigned; I was alive, I was shaking. Seconds later, we entered the supernatural, fiery cloud. I could feel the grip of the tires on the sand diminish instantly, and the winds began to violently shake the truck in every direction. Visibility was almost nil, and Mangusio slowed down. We were now driving carefully: the other truck couldn't have been far ahead, and we didn't want to hit it.

I had seen desert winds—gales that lifted up the sand—but a real sandstorm was another thing entirely. I felt like I was on Mars. The colors of the world flicked wildly from yellow to ochre. The sun, which was trying to poke through the sphere of sand that had swallowed us, tinted the blur of magma fantastic shades. We were in the middle of nowhere, under an enormous dome. I was fascinated; I had never seen anything like it in my life.

We drove through the Martian storm for at least an hour, and all the while I felt like an awestruck child. I wanted to stay in that bubble forever, on that planet where the wind howled its rebellion, subduing our vehicle. It was magical because it was exactly how I felt inside. I understood the storm; it was a reflection of myself.

I can only imagine the look on my face, my hands and my face glued to the window, eyes wide. I didn't dare blink; I didn't want to miss a second of the show. I was trying to absorb these visions to keep them in my memory and in my heart forever.

The dome of sand eventually thinned, and the sun managed to get through, drawing in threads of light. The other truck gradually rematerialized, barely a yard ahead of us. How could Mangusio have followed his companions so closely, without being able to see anything? It was beyond comprehension, one of the many secrets of the desert people.

Everything seemed surreal and muddled; I couldn't believe that I'd left the women's camp just a day earlier. Time shifts so drastically in the desert and it's so relative that I felt trapped in its enormous hourglass. Now I had lived through a storm inside the hourglass itself, with time going round and round.

Mangusio motioned for me to roll down my window so we could get some air now that the storm was behind us, and we continued north. The sun was beginning to curve down toward the horizon; the men would soon be looking for a place to spend the night. The two vehicles separated, each looking for the best hiding place. It was a race against time. The other truck found a spot before Mangusio, and circled back to guide us to the standing stone where we finally stopped. I set up my blanket on the rocks while the men made a fire and prepared food.

Night was falling. I was still shivering at the thought of what I had experienced that day.

What a storm. What an incredible planet!

Patience

In the distance the sands rose up aloft,
Slid toward me like a moving wall
And slowly too the wind started to shift
Enfolding me in its protective swell.

Wreathing the wind with its desiccation,
The desert danced a scene sublime.
Sand dove and flew, a bold orchestration
That drew me into the prison of time.

The sun maundered on, fastidious
And light, its madness blinding.
The squall blew on, oblivious
To me as I tossed in its frenzied leaping.

Patient as a stray feather, I was pinned
To the ground, my eyes closed
Against time and the dizzying wind.
I implored the desert not to take my soul.

PART VII

The Tuareg People

CAPTIVITY: DAY 244 TO DAY 415

26

Ball-Buster the Groundhog

THE FIRST GLOW of dawn was barely visible, and the earth was waking from sleep, a sleep made restless by its own nightlife. A faint horizontal light spread quietly in the sky, as if the planet was slowly opening its eyes.

The mujahideen were performing wudu, cleansing their bodies before offering their prayers to Allah in low voices. My dreams were entangled in the mists of reality, and I could hear the men in the background preparing for the first prayer of the day. I wrapped the blanket around myself a little tighter; I wasn't ready to get up quite yet. I wanted to enjoy the last few minutes of the night with my eyes closed before facing another day.

Mangusio cleared his throat, the signal to leave. I would be alone with him: the other men wouldn't be coming. I expected that Mangusio would hand me over to another team. I never stayed with one man for long. Come to think of it, I had never been alone with a mujahid.

I was right. No sooner had we driven a few miles than my driver stopped. Then he motioned for me to get out of the vehicle and crouch under a bush while he contacted someone on his walkie-talkie. Shortly afterwards, three motorbikes arrived and stopped on the other side of the bush where I was hiding. The men had no idea I was there.

Mangusio chatted with them for a while before coming back to me. He told me to get back into the truck, and we followed the three motorcyclists to their camp. Take your things and climb out, Mangusio said. In handing me over to the Tuareg, he had fulfilled his mission. He left immediately; no doubt he had a long way to go.

The Tuareg seemed happy about my arrival. They immediately pointed to a spot in the shade of a tree where I could wait. Wait for the day to pass. Wait for days to pass, without end.

The Tuareg group was much smaller than the others—only the three men. The boss was a tall, well-built man. His skin was dark, between brown and black. He was missing some teeth. He was strict: I was not allowed to get up except to relieve myself, as close to the camp as possible. There must have been a town or villages nearby, because these men were much more cautious than those in the dunes, where there hadn't been a living soul for hundreds of miles.

I nicknamed this boss Ball-Buster the Groundhog, because I could never do anything when he was around. He just wanted me to stay completely hidden. At least at the women's camp in the desert I was allowed to walk around a bit, to cook. The man reminded me of a groundhog too because of the way he came out of his hole to check on me or to make sure I was tucked away. Still, he was nice enough. At first, he came to bring me a glass of tea every day, sometimes even several times a day. It was the first time I had been given so much attention, and something akin to respect.

The glasses the Tuareg use hold about two ounces, but they only fill them halfway with tea, because the drink is like a bomb. To prepare the tea, the desert men let it brew in a teapot over coals until it's bitter, and then cut the taste by adding a ton of sugar. A single sip is enough to expand your taste buds... or knock them out.

I remember the day Ball-Buster got his nickname; it was as if life were winking at me. For dinner he brought me taguella, a typical Tuareg dish, this time with the half-testicle of a goat on top of the mountain of bread crumbled and soaked in a goat-fat sauce. That day, the testicle was both a source of protein for my body and a source of inspiration to baptize the man who'd cooked it.

The second man I called Mange-Tout because one day he handed me a bowl of food and said, "*Mange tout!*" I had never heard him speak French before and I don't know where he got the phrase, but I think he thought I was too skinny. After that, whenever he brought me food, he would repeat the words, telling me to eat it all, puffing out his cheeks, as if he was encouraging me to put on weight. Mange-Tout was not an energetic man; he was actually kind of lazy, but he smiled and laughed a lot. He didn't look mean, even with the Kalashnikov in his hand. He was the nicest, and the least credible, of the bandits.

The third man was older than the other two, and rather sickly. He coughed and sneezed all day long, and he didn't move around much. I was always kind of afraid that he wouldn't make it through the night. I named him Sneezy.

Ball-Buster the Groundhog was as good as three guards. Every time I looked at him, he was watching me. If he thought I was going to the toilet too far from the camp, he followed me like a shadow. On the other hand, Mange-Tout and Sneezy were worth about half a guard between them; the three of them formed a rather off-kilter team.

For Whom the Dinner Bell Tolls

APRIL 7, 2019
111th day in captivity

Dearest guests, come sit at our feet
And feast on our delicacies.
Here at the inn of the Hobbling Sheep
Bland and insipid is our specialty!

Do try the rice on a layer of pasta,
Our signature noodles in sand velouté.
We'll spoil you—come on, trust us,
Come sit at our table, what do you say…

The all-you-can-eat of the desert awaits,
Course upon course of grit in your teeth.
It gets everywhere, not just on your plate.
Think—oh, just think of the dunes you will eat.

Here you will dine in the utmost repose;
Our sommeliers are armed to the teeth.
Sometimes they shoot (you know how it goes),
But please let us show you your seat.

[27]

The Flood

IT WAS AUGUST; the rainy season would last until mid-September. It rained much more abundantly in the north, and Ball-Buster the Groundhog had gone to the trouble to build me a little shelter out of stems of euphorbia—a pretty plant that thrives in poor, arid soil, though you have to beware of its sap, which is an irritant, and poisonous. Ball-Buster had also intertwined leafy acacia branches to fashion me a screen against the sun. The rainy season in West Africa is typically marked by violent thunderstorms that burst intermittently, with the sky a sunny blue between storms. I stayed at the camp for two weeks. That was the only time the Tuareg built me a shelter. After that, with them, I had no shelter, no tent against the weather. They would simply point to a tree, and I followed its shadow throughout the day to protect myself a little from the scorching sun between storms.

In most Islamic societies, women and men are normally separated, but at night, so that my wardens could keep a close eye on me, I had to sleep next to them. I would go over to them at dusk, returning to my tree before daybreak. We slept out, beneath the stars, because it was easier to go unnoticed that way, without a tent, camouflaged in nature. When I'd arrived, the men had given me clothes as brown as wood, and a forest-green scarf; I looked like a plant. The Tuareg are masters in the art of concealment.

The rainy season made it a little easier for them to get water. They didn't have to go too far to find it. It was usually collected at the camp site, in the depressions created by the heavy rains. One morning, after diluting some powdered milk in my sandy, dirty water, I found a surprise: a little tadpole! It wriggled its body in my glass, probably startled to be swimming in milk. Good thing I saw it, otherwise it would have been breakfast.

We also saw a lot of big toads during the rainy season. Sometimes at night I would feel a heaviness moving over my body or jumping on my face. The toads were easy to recognize in the dark because of their weight and their cool, slimy skin. They jumped on me because I was part of their nocturnal environment, a small hill on their terrain, an obstacle breathing in and breathing out.

After the first rainstorm, Mange-Tout gave me a large plastic sheet with holes in it to protect myself and my belongings during the storms. My shelter was handy, but it was in a groove that filled up with water. When there was a heavy downpour, I had to take all my things out and put them on a small rise a few steps away. I used the plastic to try to keep my stuff dry, though it wasn't terribly useful in the end. The location of my shelter had been rather poorly chosen; I think Ball-Buster had just made sure to hide me in a hole.

There was one rainfall so powerful and heavy it stands out even now in my mind. One day, I hadn't been paying attention, and I didn't see that a river had formed tremendously quickly. Without warning, a rush of water from who knows where poured into my shelter. I grabbed my bag of blankets and my mat to save them from the flood. I fled to the nearest rise, where I tried to protect my things under the plastic, but the damage was done. I was soaked to the bone, my scarf stuck to my face, staining my skin green.

We were in a wadi, a small sanctuary where scraps of greenery clung, sinking roots into the sand. The water had come up in a flash, and now I was stuck on the hillock. I couldn't stay there for long—the water kept rising. I didn't want to be swept away by the flood and, desperate, I decided to try to cross. I took a deep inhale and waded into the water up to my waist. I clumsily tried to keep my bags above the surface, but it was almost impossible. At one point, one of my feet got stuck in the mud and in trying to free it I lost my sandal.

The holes in the plastic were getting bigger and bigger, my makeshift bags were tearing, and I was half submerged, my face smeared with green dye.

I shouted to alert the men. "My sandal! My sandal!"

Sneezy spotted my runaway sandal, which was being tossed about in the water, and he jumped in to catch it. What a hero! The other two laughed at the whole ridiculous spectacle.

My solitary sandal was now safe in the old man's hands, and I was able to cross the wadi, hoping that my bags would hold up. My guards were already on the riverbank when I climbed up. I put my bags down on the ground, finally able to breathe. It seemed absurd to have wrapped my things in plastic to protect them from the rain, when everything was soaked.

Already darkness lurked. The wind whipped at me, and I shivered in my wet clothes. That night I wrapped myself in my water-logged blanket. I wished the world would just stand still for a moment. If only I could lift my head out of the blankets and plastic and shout *STOP!* at life, and if only life might listen. I wished for some respite, a bit of time to fall asleep, to escape reality and find myself in dreamland. But the rain didn't stop, and the wind chilled me to the bone as it snuck through the holes in the plastic sheeting. I didn't sleep well that night. Dreamland didn't want me.

The next morning, my muscles were tight and tense. I'd been shivering all night, and all I wanted was to see the sun. The sun and I had a love–hate relationship during my time in Africa: on cold nights I dreamed of it, and during the day, in the stifling heat, I wanted it to disappear forever.

Bad things seldom happen alone, and that morning an army of humongous ants attacked me. I hadn't noticed the night before that I'd been lying next to an anthill. That morning I found out that an ant attack hurts. Badly! At dawn, hordes of insects invaded my blanket and ravaged my skin. The bites were torture! I squirmed like I have never squirmed before, trying to rid myself of all those relentless little soldiers. I smacked at them, decapitating them, but their heads hung in my flesh, giving off a foul smell. It was a real massacre, a war without mercy; by moving into their territory without their permission, I had become their enemy. At the end of the battle, I had to pick out the heads one by one from my skin, shuddering with disgust. But the poor ants had lost their lives. I felt a bit cruel, but when you're attacked, you have to defend yourself.

I couldn't see the faces of the three men lying next to me, but I could feel their eyes on me. We wouldn't speak of the ant attack, of course; everything is too complicated to explain when you don't know the other's language.

I remember another day when I had to call Ball-Buster the Groundhog to the rescue. I had seen a snake chasing a lizard right in front of me. When the snake spotted me, it slithered under the tangle of branches and weeds that had accumulated at the foot of my acacia tree after the floods.

I tried to explain to Ball-Buster that a snake was hiding there under the debris. I drew winding tracks in the sand and tried to imitate the sound of a snake slithering. Ball-Buster looked at me, then at the nest of branches. To make sure he'd understood, he crouched down in turn to trace a line on the sand and mimicked the sound of the snake. I nodded. Ball-Buster surprised me with two words of French. "*Pas bon!*" he exclaimed, and stood up, examining the ground around my tree. Not good, he repeated before returning to his shelter. I waited patiently a little further out in the blazing sun, thinking that Ball-Buster would come back with some kind of tool to dislodge the snake, but I think he preferred to rely on the will of Allah.

There wasn't much I could do—I wasn't allowed away from the tree, so I too had to submit to the will of Allah and go back to my strip of shade under the acacia.

Thankfully, I never saw the snake again.

The Wildflower

SEPTEMBER 29, 2019
286th day in captivity

Side by side
We watched the devastation.
Alone in the landslide
Of earth's lamentation.

I found a little wildflower
And sat to keep it company.
Both of us in the rain shower,
Wilting from the intensity.

But the flower withered and sagged,
It smelled like nothing now.
I held its thin stem in my hand
And cradled it, gentle and slow—

I placed the flower back on the ground,
Lay down to keep it company.
I watched its petals blowing around.
Now I was alone in the immensity.

[28]

Solitude

I SPENT SIX MONTHS with the Tuareg. I was separated first from Luca on March 4, 2019, and then from the women on August 15. I was now a woman alone, held hostage by extremists. It's hard for me to put into words the loneliness I felt day after day. I didn't know what to think about or how to occupy my mind. Over the course of a year, I had time to go through my life, my dreams, my thoughts at least a thousand times. It was too much. There was no one to talk to; I couldn't even remember what my voice sounded like. Sometimes, when I went to relieve myself, I would find pretty rocks on the ground and bring them back to admire their colors and shapes. Sometimes I balanced them on top of each other, but Ball-Buster didn't like that. I think he was afraid it was witchcraft, so I had to give up even that pastime, that meditation.

I didn't often come into contact with my wardens, which was fine, because I didn't particularly like their presence, though I have to say that the first group was quite funny, especially Mange-Tout. He was able to shift the energy of a particular situation by himself, just because he was nice and silly. Mange-Tout wasn't a very convincing villain, and that rubbed off on the other two.

Even before I was brought north, I rarely saw the guards. With Luca, and with the women too, we'd had the freedom to prepare our own meals, which greatly limited the need for contact. They just kept an eye on us and brought us our water rations. With the Tuareg it was different: they cooked and brought me my food.

Now I ate more or less the same thing twice a day for six months. The typical Tuareg dish, taguella, is made of durum wheat bread baked under the sand. When they have mutton or goat, they simmer a broth with the meat and fat and pour it over the crumbled bread. They add oil and a little salt and let the crumb soak up the sauce, adding pieces of meat on top. When there was no meat, they added oil and salt to the bread, or sometimes milk and sugar.

One to three times a week, I was also entitled to a pasta dish. The Tuareg cooked pasta in mutton broth for an hour or two until it had absorbed all the liquid. It was basically a pasta pie, the noodles all fused together—so much so that you could slice it with a knife. Their pasta is not terribly al dente.

Mange-Tout used to make me laugh when he brought me my bowl of food, smiling and announcing proudly, taguella, as if I didn't already know what I was going to be eating. The dish was neither good nor bad. It was simple and didn't taste like much, except when the meat was rancid or when they used tripe, which was disgusting. When Mange-Tout brought me tea, he would say, ataï!—tea in Tamasheq. He had a rather naïve disposition, but he was always proud of what he had to offer.

The other two, Ball-Buster and Sneezy, were a bit more formal, but still respectful. They were committed to doing their job well, and I never felt any disdain from them, even though to them I was an infidel. In their minds they were doing something good; they were proud to be good mujahideen, to fight in the way of Allah. The men believe that by carrying out specific tasks, according to their interpretation of the Quran, they will have a privileged place alongside their god.

There were two groups of Tuareg guards, who took turns at each full moon. The second group had four men: two in their twenties and two in their forties or fifties. Papadou was the leader.

With them, there were no smiles accompanying the *ataï* and the taguella. When they were in charge, I had to constantly stare at the ground. One of the youngsters, whom I had nicknamed the Rooster, had warned me. It was important for him to let me know that he was superior to me. I figured that this was his battle, not mine. So, to placate the Rooster, I looked at his feet rather than his face when he handed me my food. I decided maybe he wanted me to look down because he thought he had good-looking feet.

My loneliness was deeper when I was in the care of the second, unfriendly group. I didn't speak, and I had only my shadow to keep me company. We stayed next to each other in silence. I was forbidden from walking around, and my muscles atrophied. My morale was low. I lay on the ground all day long; my only occupation was opening and closing my eyes. The days seemed endless, and I was so hot under my long clothes and scarf that I felt like I was suffocating. I was listless; I had no stimulation whatsoever. I felt as if I had been lost in suspended time, prostrate in the middle of nowhere. I barely had enough energy to sit up.

One day, it occurred to me to do yoga to tone up my legs and arms, lying down so that the men wouldn't suspect anything. What a gift! Why hadn't I had the courage to start sooner? I slowly began to rebuild my life and my spirits, thanks to the endorphins that proved a real miracle cure. I did one session of yoga in the morning, before the sun was completely up; otherwise it was too hot. And I did another in the evening, when the sun went down and the heat was a bit more tolerable.

When people ask me how I kept from going crazy, I tell them, yoga! If a day went by that I didn't get to do my sessions, whether from a lack of motivation or because I felt sick, my spirits were immediately dampened. I used this antidote until the end—my shadow and me, doing yoga together.

I had also made a friend, Scarlet, a beautiful spider as big as the palm of my hand, with a slender body. I didn't know if it was

poisonous, or if its bite might be deadly; I never asked the mujahideen because if they had known about the spider they would
have killed it. Yet I wasn't afraid of Scarlet, who spent most of her
time in the middle of her web, moving only to devour the insects
she trapped. In any case, by that point I didn't care about anything,
even death.

I liked Scarlet. I often did my yoga next to her, so that we were
both busy doing our own thing, without disturbing each other. But
one morning, I found her web empty, destroyed, which seemed
tragic. My companion had disappeared, leaving me alone with my
shadow once more.

Ghost Ship

Bells echoed through the streets,
The muffled toll of fate.
It was time to go aboard and meet
My shadow standing there in wait.

I walked onto the ghost ship
In the queue of the damned,
My crime held softly on my lips:
To slaughter with the lambs.

They cast off the moorings
And wind caught in tattered sails.
In the gloom the ship was fading,
Skirting land where memory fails.

I saw my shadow staring at me,
Searching for hope in my soul.
I held its hand in mine, trembling at the sea—
How vast it must be, how cold.

For a while silence walked beside
Though I wished it would keep its distance.
I had to believe it wanted us to survive;
I never asked for its presence.

In the end I think the ship vanished...
I could see we were going nowhere,
Faces drifting in the mist.
And my shadow left me there.

[29]

Baba

At the end of October, life gave me a great gift, a joy I hadn't been expecting at all. To tell the truth, I had two surprises that month. The first was more mundane, but the second seemed to come straight from the fount of universal love. It gave me new strength that would allow me to hold on a little better to the hope that had become so fragile—my dream of going back home one day and finding all the people I loved.

You may wonder how I knew that it was the end of October. The answer is simple: every morning, on each new day, I spoke the name of the month and the date out loud. I had learned this from the women, and it worked. The women never lost track of the days and hadn't for years. Linda would announce the new date in the morning, and Elisabeth and I confirmed its accuracy, assuring her that she had not made a mistake. Around December, however, I got tired of naming days and dates. I no longer saw the point, so I just stopped, and gradually I lost track of time.

The day of the shift change had arrived: I knew because the moon would be full that night. I waited patiently to see which men would replace Papadou's group. Would they be decent? Would they look at me as a heathen who wasn't worth much more than a stone? Lying on the ground with my eyes closed, I dreaded what would happen next.

The motorbikes arrived. One, two, three. The newcomers chatted around the fire with Papadou and his men, no doubt having tea before the changing of the guard.

Soon after, I heard footsteps coming closer. I knew it had to be the leader of the group coming to introduce himself, so I sat up to greet him. The man was tall and looked muscular. He leaned toward me and pulled down his scarf to reveal his toothless grin. Ball-Buster the Groundhog! Until my time with the Tuareg, I'd never had the same group of guards twice. I greeted him with a funny smile and he handed me a glass of tea: "*Ataï!*" I drank it in one gulp, with pleasure, and gave him back his glass, thanking him. Papadou and his men left, and I was again in the care of a nicer team. I was relieved because I knew that these three men would behave kindly toward me.

Two days later, I was once again lying on the ground with my eyes closed, wishing that the day would go by as quickly as possible, when suddenly I heard the sound of an engine in the distance. I opened my eyes again and turned my head to see who was coming. A motorbike stopped alongside me, and a man in khaki camouflage got off. Since when did visitors come to see me without going through the chief? The man greeted me and handed me a red envelope with my name in big letters: EDITH. What a shock! Everything around me vanished instantly: all I could see was a hand holding a red envelope. My heart nearly leapt out of my chest. I wasn't at all prepared to receive such a treasure. I immediately opened the envelope, though it had already been opened. As the man stood and watched in silence, I took out two letters and three photos. I had tears in my eyes, but I tried to hide them, because I didn't want to show emotion to the man in khaki. I read the two beautiful letters, written by old friends, friends from Canada! How had the letters reached me? I didn't know, but they were a breath of happiness.

I looked at the three photos. Two of them were pictures of me. The first one had been taken by Luca on Vancouver Island. I was sitting on the trunk of a massive fallen redwood—a majestic tree that can grow over three hundred feet high and a hundred feet around. I was smiling broadly, proud of my colossal wooden chair. The second photo had been taken on a mountain near Maligne Lake in Jasper National Park. I realized that they weren't just two pictures of me; they were pictures of me in Canada. I wished I were still sitting on that redwood tree, smiling at Luca. I dreamed of going back to climb that mountain, to breathe in that fresh air that tasted like freedom. In the photos, I was still innocent. That smile revealed a young woman full of dreams and courage; it was the smile of a woman who has no idea of what lies ahead. It had been so long since I had felt such a sense of joy and well-being.

The man in khaki was bothering me, though; I couldn't daydream comfortably with him watching me. I turned my attention to the third photo, and recognized my father! He and I had been arm wrestling, and the photo, taken in the heat of the action, showed our faces, straining with the effort and laughing. It was a beautiful picture. I took it as a message to stay strong. Yes, I had to be strong. I sighed and held the photo to my heart. The man, who was still standing in front of me, pointed at the picture, which I wanted to protect from all the evil in the world.

"*Baba*?" he asked me.

"Sorry?"

He wanted to see the picture I was pressing against my chest. I hesitated, then showed it to him reluctantly. He pointed to my father and repeated his question.

"*Baba*?"

I finally understood what he was asking.

"Yes, my papa!" I replied, pointing to my father.

Then the man pointed to the woman in the photo.

"Mama?" he asked.

He thought it was my mother! I shook my head and pointed my index finger at myself.

"No, that's me."

He simply nodded; he seemed thoughtful.

I had noticed that the envelope had been opened before the visitor handed it to me, but also that it had been thicker: I could tell by the folds in the edges, which didn't match the contents. I found it curious that I had received letters from my friends, but not from my mother, sister, or father. Perhaps they had been taken out of the envelope. I knew my family must be working hard to find me, but I didn't know what they were doing. I didn't know what the Canadian government was doing either. Surely they wouldn't pay a ransom to terrorists. Maybe they were looking for me? All those drones flying around in the sky gave me an infinitesimal hope that I might one day be found.

My poor family! My poor friends! They must all have been so worried. One day, I'd wanted to send them a letter, and I had asked Eyeglasses, the man who had made videos for our governments and families, to do me the favor when he came to make a video with Elisabeth. He said he would try to pass on my message. I didn't really believe he would, but at least I tried to reassure my people that I was alive, that I was thinking of them and that I loved them. When I got back to Canada, I wasn't too shocked to learn that the letter had never arrived. I also found out that everyone had gone out of their way to send me letters, food, photos, and even a pair of glasses. My mother told me that she had a bad dream one night and knew right away that I couldn't see, so she'd had a pair of glasses made, hoping that they would reach me.

Ball-Buster appeared suddenly. He wanted to see the letters I had gotten, and I showed them to him because I trusted him, at least a little. Until then, he had never betrayed me; he had never taken what was mine. He looked at the letters curiously and handed them back to me with a smile. I couldn't help crying; the tears were getting harder to choke back. Ball-Buster saw me weeping, and touched his heart with a smile. I did the same in reply. Yes, the letters had touched my heart, he understood that.

Ball-Buster pointed to the woman in the pictures, and I explained that it was me. *Canada!* I added, pointing proudly to the trees, mountains, and lakes of Jasper. He nodded, then turned his attention to the man in the third photo, waiting for my response.

"Papa," I said, wondering if he would know the word.

"*Baba*," he echoed, shaking his head again and pressing a hand to his heart.

The tears flowed freely as I imitated his gesture, as if I were his reflection. I love my father, and the picture meant the world to me.

What a lovely surprise I had that day.

Yet Ball-Buster was true to his nickname. He came back to see me the next day and pointed his index finger at the letters I kept rereading.

"*Fini*," he said in French. No more.

"Finished?" I repeated.

I didn't understand what he was asking, but he insisted: he wanted me to give him my letters. I was forced to obey. He smiled at me once more and left with my treasure. I was stunned... My letters! I never saw them again. I can assure you that I hid my poems well after that; I always wrote in secret. I realized that I couldn't trust the man after all.

By that point in my captivity, there was no ink left in my pen, though I could use it to scratch words into a piece of cardboard. I could read my poems by rubbing some ash on the cardboard. It was a laborious technique, but those poems were the only valuable thing I had.

It's a good thing that Ball-Buster never asked me to hand over my three precious photos. I would have fought for them; I would never have let him burn them.

Curiously, the picture of my *baba* and me was very popular among the mujahideen. Any man who came to meet me would ask to see it. Invariably, as soon as I took it out, they would point to my father and say, *Baba!* Perhaps the men also had children. In any case, my father must have touched them, because after seeing the photo, I sometimes caught them looking at me tenderly. *Baba,* they would say.

The Letter

231st day in captivity

The wind that morning, impish bandit
Woke gently and went on a tear,
Rustled the bushes and shook out the fruit,
And played like a child in my hair.

Perfumed with scents from afar,
It lavished the autumn collection.
It laid red leaves on my satin garb
And tousled my locks with affection.

But the wind snatched the letter I grasped
And flew from the scene of the crime.
I ran after the thief and shouted, aghast—
The wind had stolen what was mine.

It whistled a little under the train,
Whipping out of control in the crash,
The letter—my letter—escaped but in vain,
Scraps fluttered like ash.

[30]

Sculpture

AFTER THREE AND a half months, Papadou's group, which was back, made me change camp. I had never spent so much time in one place. The guards I'd had before the Tuareg used to move me with every new team.

I inspected my new home, walking around my new tree. I noticed that the soil was different: it was no longer exactly sand. In fact, if you mixed it with water, it compacted, which meant I could make sculptures out of it. I had a sudden artistic impulse to embellish my new home. I also found some colorful rocks around my tree that I could use to decorate my domain. I arranged red, pink, ochre, and crystal-blue stones in a spiral, finishing the pattern with ivory-colored shards. I was happy; I felt like I was living in a Zen space; it had good energy. I began to work on a sculpture that I would place at the entrance of my home.

I spent three days on the piece. I put all my time into it—and God knows how much time I had. I created a man's face, life-sized, emerging from the earth. I wanted it to be realistic; I even gave him eyelids. I liked the idea of him being the guardian of the sun, so I carved a wide sun on the ground. There! My acacia was probably the most beautifully decorated tree in the desert.

I had named one of the men in the second group Amano-Pierre. He was in his early twenties, the youngest of the four. It was mainly him who took care of me. He would bring me water to bathe, hence the name Amano: *aman* means water in Tamasheq. The other part of his name came from the fact that he used to throw stones at camels and donkeys to make them leave. He was the only person I had encountered who used that somewhat barbaric technique, yet he was kind and considerate to me. He wasn't like the Rooster; he didn't feel the need to dominate me, and never asked me to lower my gaze to his feet.

The day had come to reveal my sun guardian to Amano-Pierre. The men couldn't see the sculpture from where they normally stood, so when he brought me my food, I had to direct his gaze with my finger.

"*Ma-dar-tolahad, labas?*" I said first, greeting him in Tamasheq and asking whether he was well.

When I showed Amano-Pierre my sculpture, his face tensed. He looked shaken. He immediately turned to me so that I would explain what it was. Seeing his confusion, I tried to make him understand, by showing him the clay, that he had nothing to fear, that it was only a harmless sculpture. Amano-Pierre gave me my bowl of food and turned away, still flustered. Maybe when he saw my work, the face surrounded by feathers, the sun, and all those spiraling stones, he was afraid of some witchcraft. The Tuareg were deeply frightened of sorcery.

The next day, the team leader came to bring me my lunch. Young Amano must have told him that there was a face at the foot of my tree, because as soon as he arrived he looked in that direction. This was the man I had nicknamed Papadou, because I was sure he had children. He looked like a father. My group of guards was divided into two: the good guys and the beasts. The two good guys were Amano-Pierre and Papadou.

Papadou asked me with gestures what the ornaments meant, but it was difficult to explain. I also tried to convey to him that it was only a harmless sculpture. He hesitated, then gave me my food and left, looking doubtful.

On the third day, it was the turn of the chief's second-in-command to come. Usually, he wasn't particularly mean or kind; he was content to give me my food without even looking at me. He had never spoken to me, not even in Tamasheq, but now, like the others, he wanted to understand the meaning of my sculpture. I tried once again to explain, but he didn't seem convinced. He left without saying anything.

My artistic works had disturbed the mujahideen. Secretly, I felt a certain pleasure at seeing the fear in their eyes. I even thought it might work in my favor. In any case, I was sure I hadn't heard the last of this.

The next day, the Rooster came to bring me my ration. I was looking forward to his reaction. When he pointed to the sun guardian's face, I just smiled. The Rooster motioned to me that I should destroy my sculpture, but I made it clear that I would not obey. As I had told the others, I reassured him: he had nothing to fear from this earthen face. With fear in his eyes, he handed me my bowl of taguella, and again he signaled that I should demolish my work, walking away before I had a chance to answer.

Those who know me know that I wouldn't have destroyed my sun guardian, just like that. But the matter was far from settled.

Madness and the Statue in the Sand

I saw a statue in this other land
Across a border undefined.
Without knowing, I crossed and found
This warrior from another time.

I heard madness scampering
And shouted, *stay away from me!*
I fell to my knees, keening,
My body wounded and lonely.

I ducked behind the statue's shield
Like a soldier frozen in battle.
I wanted to be concealed
But the statue just stood, inscrutable.

Madness prowled all around us,
The wind whistled into the fray,
And the unhinged laugh of madness
Spurred the sand to fly and spray.

Madness inched ever closer,
Admiring the figures of sand it had crafted.
The woman, exhausted, begged the warrior
For help, lost in a desert of fables.

[31]

Rebellion

IT WAS DECEMBER. It had been a year since I'd been kidnapped. Need I say that I was royally fed up? Luca and I had been separated for nine months, and I had no idea what had become of him. Was he alive? Had he returned to Italy? Had he tried to escape? So many questions rattled through my head. As for me, I had been in the north of Mali, in the hands of the Tuareg, for four months, alone, forced to remain immobile day and night. I had had it up to there!

It wasn't yet time for my meal, yet I could hear footsteps. It was the Rooster, visiting me to check if I had carried out his orders from the day before. He wanted to see the ground cleared of my artwork, but I was gratified to show him that my sun warrior was intact, and more beautiful than ever. Clearly outraged by my refusal to comply, he turned back. With a small, satisfied smile, I listened: the Rooster was not at all pleased. I could hear him shouting in the distance. The voices of Papadou, his second-in-command, and Amano-Pierre threaded through the confusion. How would it all turn out?

More footsteps. Amano-Pierre: they had sent the youngest to do the dirty work. He stopped at the foot of my tree, looked at my sculptures and, pointing to my sun, asked me what it was.

"*Tafouk*," I replied in Tamasheq—the sun.

He said no, I was not allowed to carve a star: it was forbidden in Islam. He'd caught me off guard; I'd been expecting to have to fight to save the bust. I could sacrifice the sun if that was the problem. I found his request much more reasonable than the Rooster's, so I scratched out the celestial body to please him, and to calm the others. In the end, my sun guardian would be the guardian of compromise. Amano-Pierre left, looking relieved.

I almost liked him. I thought he was smarter than the Rooster, and more courageous. He had stood up for me many times. For example, on days when there was hardly any water and I asked him for some to wash myself, I could hear him in the distance arguing with the others on my behalf. He almost always came back with a little water, smiling. There is one week every month when a woman needs more water than usual, though any mention of anything to do with menstruation was unacceptable. It was never an easy time for me; I always had to use my imagination to sort things out without making it obvious.

I remember one time, one story among many others: in February, after fleeing into the desert with the mujahideen, Luca and I had stayed for two weeks under an acacia tree waiting for Barbarossa to return. I happened to be menstruating, and all we had on us were the few clothes we had been wearing all along. In February, after sunset, the temperature in the desert drops dramatically and can reach the freezing mark. We didn't have warm clothes or blankets, and we were freezing. On the first day of my period, I had to tell Luca that I didn't know what to use to soak up the blood. And we were allowed so little water that I didn't see how I would cope.

"Take this," he said, handing me his only pair of socks. "And I'll ask them for more water, don't worry."

"No, Luca! Your feet will freeze tonight!"

He insisted. Did I have a choice? Heroic and chivalrous, Luca had bailed me out once more. And sure enough, his feet were frozen. Later, with the women, I had been given scraps of cloth with which I had been able to make something more absorbent.

Back to the sculpture debacle: two days after I'd destroyed my sun, there was some movement in the camp. The chief and the second-in-command left the camp, leaving me with the two young men. They were sitting around the fire drinking tea, and I could hear them talking stubbornly. Clearly, they were at odds with each other. From the tone of the discussion, I had the feeling that Amano-Pierre was trying to prevent the other man from doing something.

My hunch must have been correct, because the Rooster strode over to me a few moments later, his chest puffed up, with an acacia root in his mouth. Standing at the foot of my tree, he pointed to the sculpture and ordered me to destroy it. What? I was incensed! I wasn't going to destroy my poor sculpture just because the Rooster's pride had been hurt when I agreed to erase my sun to please Amano. I motioned to him that I would not, and took the trouble once again to show him that my sculpture was harmless. He gestured again with his hand, as if to crush my work disdainfully. Out of the question! Who did he think he was? Did he want me to believe that in Papadou's absence he was in charge?

I realized that I had to choose between two possibilities: I could refuse to destroy my sculpture, in which case I would be guilty and punished for disobedience, or I could get the Rooster in trouble for having given me orders without his boss's knowledge.

The role of the guards is to hold hostages captive while the leaders try to negotiate with governments. The hostages must be able to eat and drink; they must not run away or be seen. I had some value to them, otherwise they wouldn't have fed me for a year, and they wouldn't have assigned so many men to guard me. I would have been curious to know how much money they had spent on little old me, including flour and meat, and how much they expected to get. War is expensive, and they used us as bargaining chips.

The guards' mission was to preserve the market value of their property—in this case, me. My decision was made: I stood up and smashed the sculpture with a big kick. The Rooster's eyes widened. He hadn't expected such wrath from me. Then I grabbed my bowl of food and flung it away like a Frisbee. The Rooster got the message: I was going to stop eating, and thus jeopardize their mission. He ran back to Amano-Pierre with a hangdog look. I could hear them arguing.

A few minutes later, Amano stood before me. He pointed to the bowl lying on the ground and motioned for me to go pick it up. Good! I was suddenly allowed to go for a walk, and I would take the opportunity to stretch my legs a bit. I was fed up with these men who treated me like an animal, and I wanted to teach the Rooster a lesson...and I was prepared to go on a hunger strike again. I had paid the price by smashing my sculpture, but I wanted respect. Since I'd been held prisoner, I had analyzed the men pretty extensively, and I knew their weak points. The ball was in my court.

At dinner time, the Rooster sent Amano to get my bowl and fill it with food. I made it clear to Amano that I was done, I would never eat again, that I was very angry. He left looking glum. The two young men were getting nervous: their leader had ordered them to look after me for two days, and now, through their recklessness, they had ruined everything. It was a serious matter for them not to be able to make their hostage obey. I remembered Barbarossa inviting us to eat by threatening us with his Kalashnikov.

The next day I heard the two young men talking again. Around noon, the Rooster came to bring me some food. Inside I was smiling: the Rooster had lost his bluster and his pride, and I could see in his eyes that he was afraid of me. I stood up and signaled to him to back off immediately, that he was on my territory and that I would not eat. I even puffed out my chest to intimidate him, as he had done the day before. If he was looking for a fight, he would find a formidable, desperate opponent.

I laughed a little inside because the attitude was so contrary to my personality. But I wanted to destabilize the Rooster and show him the consequences of his mistake. He wasn't so brave; I'd even venture that he was afraid. He turned and almost ran away. Good. It was satisfying to have regained some control over a tiny piece of my life. I didn't have much room to maneuver, but rebelling on my own terms kept my mind busy, and it felt great.

At the next mealtime, Amano appeared. I tried to explain to him again, using gestures and the Tamasheq words I had learned, that I would not eat any more, that I was tired of being their prisoner. I think he understood this time, because before leaving he explained that their task was to feed me and give me water. He was getting nervous: the chief would be back soon, and Amano didn't know how to regain control of the situation. Too bad for him.

After two days of absence, the second-in-command returned. I thought that the two young people would report to him immediately, and I wondered if the man, who usually ignored me, would come to me. And yes, he did come over to what I thought of as my territory. He seemed to be fully in control. It was disquieting, the way he looked at me. I didn't move; I waited. Eventually he handed me a bowl of milk, which I refused. He didn't insist, and just went back to the fire. I think they had decided to wait for the chief to come back and advise them.

Papadou returned an hour later. The four men met for tea to discuss what to do next. Shortly afterwards, with a glass of tea in hand, Papadou paid me a visit.

"*Ma-dar-tolahad, labas?*"

I refused the glass of tea he held out to me, and waited for him to come closer. He crouched down to be at my level; his eyes were full of compassion, and it shook me. With tears in my eyes, I tried to make him understand that I had been a captive for a year, that they had taken my husband away from me nine months before, that I didn't know where he was or even if he was alive, that I was going crazy with loneliness, and that all of it was inhuman.

Suddenly I fell silent, and took a deep breath. Was I ranting at nothing? How could he understand me, when he didn't speak a word of French? He took a piece of candy out of a pocket and held it out. That was when he earned the nickname Papadou: he looked like a father who no longer knows what to do to comfort his child. But moments of gentleness and compassion didn't do me any good, and I started crying even harder. It had been so long, and now that I'd opened the floodgates the tears wouldn't stop.

I refused the candy, and I said I wanted water, because water came from Allah, but I didn't want anything else. No milk, no tea, no food, and especially no treats. He offered me water to take a shower. I hesitated for a moment before accepting. Water was brought, and I went away to wash myself.

Papadou was right: the water soothed me. It always feels good to wash. A woman feels better when she is clean and perfumed like a flower.

But I wasn't going to eat.

Wild Soul

NOVEMBER 20, 2019
338th day in captivity

My soul is wild, it howls at night
And careens unchecked in my belly.
With nowhere to go, it buckles and writhes
And cries that it wants to be free.

I hear it growling in anguish,
Baring its fangs and pacing about.
I don't want my wild soul to perish—
Gnawing through my skin, it wants out.

My soul has been hurt once too often;
In my eyes it cowers in fear.
There was a time when nothing would soften
The edge of its longing and cheer.

We're both bored to death,
We've been locked in a cage.
I have a wild soul that screams for breath
And we storm together, enraged.

Crazy Eyes

WHILE I WAS washing, oblivious to what was going on, Papa-dou had made a call to solve the problem: if none of them could convince me to eat, someone else would have to do it.

The cold December wind had been blowing for a few days without letting up. Washing in such conditions, and with freezing water to boot, is unpleasant. So I was quick, and didn't use the whole gallon Amano had brought me. The rest I could save for laundry.

Even before I returned to my acacia tree, I saw a truck in the distance coming toward us. I rarely saw that kind of vehicle anymore. The Tuareg traveled by motorbike; a truck probably announced the arrival of someone more important. I suspected that the visit had to do with my hunger strike.

The Rooster and Amano quickly left the camp on their motorbikes before the truck arrived. Papadou didn't understand why I had stopped eating, but I think he blamed the two young men for the trouble. Papadou and the second-in-command welcomed the two visitors; the tension was palpable. From his manner and dress, one of them must have been a leader in the organization. The other was his driver.

It was four in the afternoon, the time of the afternoon prayer. The second-in-command called the adhan to begin the prayer and the four men performed their ablutions. Then the boss, taking the role of the imam, led the prayer in Papadou's place, indicating his status in the hierarchy.

When the prayer was over, the leader came to me. I dubbed him Crazy Eyes.

"Hello, Edith, how are you?"

It was a shock to hear him say my name.

"Fine," I replied without thinking too much about it.

"Is that so? But the men told me that you don't want to eat anything."

Crazy Eyes smiled. His French was impeccable. He knelt comfortably on the sand in front of me. I didn't trust him; there was a weird vibe about him. He had the look of a man who knows how to make people obey, whatever the cost. I tried to size him up, but I didn't know how to deal with him; I didn't know what to say.

The driver joined us, put a big box next to my mat, and at a signal from his boss he sat down on the ground. He was visibly uncomfortable, nervous, as if he was already ready to get up. He didn't dare look at me.

Crazy Eyes looked dangerous, and I thought it might be wise to abandon the role of the fighter, which I played with my wardens, and adopt the low profile of a more submissive woman.

"You've been holding me captive for a year," I said cautiously. "You separated me from my husband, and I don't even know if he is alive or..."

"I know everything," Crazy Eyes interrupted me.

It was the first time I had come across anyone who really knew what was going on. I took the opportunity to ask him the questions that had been burning on my tongue for months:

"Is Luca okay?"

"He is alive and that is all that matters. He is alive, and you are alive too."

"Has he been released?"

"He is with us," the man replied with a strange smile.

"I want to be back with him."

"I can't get you back together. However, here's what I propose: we could make a video with Luca, a video just for you, but in exchange you have to give up your hunger strike."

I was speechless. A video of Luca! I could see him alive; I could see how he was doing.

"I want to see the video!" I blurted hopefully. I've never been a very good negotiator. "When will I get it?"

"I have to send a man over there, it might take a week, but you have to start eating again, even if there is a slight delay."

"Okay!"

I accepted the deal, smiling like a child. Crazy Eyes was satisfied, and his driver suddenly relaxed. I suspected that if I hadn't accepted his proposal, he would have used another method. Seeing that I was cooperative, he pushed on.

"You will also read the Quran and learn the prayers to become a good Muslim."

I frowned. I had to be careful what I said to him.

"At the moment," I said, "I have no desire to convert to Islam, and I don't think that's why you came."

"You will become a Muslim! You will pray to Allah!"

"You know, I have respect for your religion and—"

"Respect?" he was indignant, his eyes flashing. "That's not respect! You're going to become a Muslim! If we died and both stood before God, He would ask me why I didn't convert you. What would you like me to say? That I tried, but you wouldn't listen? No! You are a disbeliever and you are an animal in the eyes of God if you refuse Islam."

I couldn't believe my ears. God would look upon my captor favorably while I, who wouldn't harm a fly, would go to hell? What a backwards mentality. The worst thing was that Crazy Eyes was absolutely convinced of what he was saying. I didn't know how to answer him; religion was a delicate matter.

"I am not an unbeliever, I believe in God," I said as diplomatically as possible. "For me, God is Life, and I give thanks for all that Life gives me."

"Yes, but our prophet, Mohammed—"

It was my turn to interrupt him.

"You speak to me of disbelief, and I tell you that I believe in Allah, in God, in Life, call it what you want, it's only a name. On the other hand, your prophet is not God, he is the founder of your religion; it's not the same thing. I am a child of God, just like you."

He raised his hand to silence me.

"First, you will eat." He explained the deal again. "Then you will receive a video from your husband. Finally, you will become a good Muslim and pray to Allah."

He then pointed to the box that his driver had placed by my mat, staring ominously into my eyes.

"The box contains date biscuits; they are for you. I am not leaving until you eat them."

I took a biscuit from the box, and replied that I would feed myself while I waited impatiently for Luca's video, but I did not expressly say that I would convert to Islam. In any event, his request wasn't open to discussion; it was simply an order.

The big boss was satisfied. Everything had gone smoothly; he hadn't been forced to lay down the law.

The woman had obeyed.

The Gods

The nectar of the gods flows forth
From where they gather in the clouds.
What goddesses sowed in the loam at their court
Unimagined grew lush and proud.

From the god of storms some lightning slipped
And split the darkness, thrilling the night.
Everyone clapped, their faces lit
In the eternal light.

The god of the night disappeared for a moment
And carved his stars, a celestial writ.
He left his trace wherever he went,
Shedding light on the world and sharing his wit.

As in a great funnel the wind poured down—
Spinning, unsure of where to begin.
The breeze fluttered a bit and looked around,
A gift of the goddess of wind.

Another picked and painted some seeds,
Tossing a few to the sky so pure.
The colors burst and the goddess's deed
Scattered and fell to unfurl.

Thus came the earth into being, from naught,
Set to spinning by the god of time.
Waves rushing in and out,
Setting music on the world's sandy spine.

Then the god of movement wove the future,
Each fate threaded along its journey.
Some went on at length, some ended sooner.
The god just smiled, benevolently.

[33]

The Video

AFTER MY THREE-DAY hunger strike, I got sick. I think my body was too weak to withstand the deprivation. The wind had been blasting day and night, and my body had no respite. I had a fever and my stomach was upset. It was a struggle to eat at all.

I was trying to make my jailers understand that this was no longer a hunger strike, that I was ill. I wanted to see Luca's video, but I couldn't hold up my end of the bargain with Crazy Eyes. In the morning, Amano brought me warm sweet milk, which was the only thing I could swallow. My condition gradually improved and after a week I started to eat a bit again—*akšu, akšu,* as they say in Tamasheq.

Around December 25—I had lost track of the days by then—an unknown motorbike appeared. For a few days now, Ball-Buster the Groundhog and his men had been back to watch me. It was Ball-Buster who welcomed the visitor. Soon after, they came over to my spot, laughing and talking loudly.

"*Ma-dar-tolahad,*" I greeted them.

The stranger smiled at me blissfully, like a child about to reveal a secret. I wondered why he was so happy to see me, and why Ball-Buster seemed so amused.

"Video!" the stranger shouted at me.

"Luca's video? Do you have Luca's video?"

Guffawing, the man signaled that he didn't understand. "Video!" he repeated, and handed me his phone. My heart was racing, blood pulsing so hard in my temples that I was dizzy. I couldn't believe it. Finally, someone had kept their word! I was going to see my Luca.

I grabbed the visitor's phone, and my eyes fell on the still image of Luca, the video waiting for me to press play. The stranger laughed again when he noticed how upset I was—I was a little afraid of what I was about to see. The man leaned over to play the video for me, and Luca came to life before my eyes. I looked at his mouth, at his eyes, his beard, his short hair, his hands—fairly clean—and his clothes, and again at his lips, moving, making sounds, but I couldn't understand what he was saying because the two men next to me were speaking so loudly. I motioned at them to be quiet. I must have looked funny, because they started laughing again. Then the stranger signaled to Ball-Buster to leave me alone, and made it clear that I could watch the video as often as I wanted before giving back his phone.

As soon as the stranger and Ball-Buster had gone back to the men's camp, I checked to see if I could call for help, but there was no signal. At least I could finally hear Luca. I started the video again: Luca didn't look bad; he was telling me that he was fine, not to worry about him, that we had to keep hope alive, that one day we would get through this. When he told me that he had converted to Islam, my heart actually stopped beating. Not a beat, not a sound; I couldn't hear anything. But why? Why had he joined their religion? I couldn't understand. I knew Luca, and I was sure he would never have converted if he didn't have a good reason to do so. Surely he had to have gotten something out of it, but why was he telling me about it in the video? Surely not just to confuse me. So then why?

Lost in thought, I didn't catch the end of the video, and went back to the beginning. Yes, Luca seemed fine and, yes, he seemed calm. He was also very handsome, I thought, he was beautiful, although the beard bothered me: it made him look like our kidnappers. He said he was learning Arabic and reading the Quran. He thought he was lucky to be able to keep his mind occupied; it kept him from going crazy. He told me that he was trying to get what he could out of this mishap, and then he said goodbye, telling me to be brave, and that he wished with all his heart that I could return to Canada soon.

That was it; the video was over. I watched it about ten times, until I knew it by heart, but I was still dumbfounded. Why had he converted to Islam?

That night was anything but restful. I squirmed under my blanket, shivering in the fierce wind and brooding over a thousand questions. I replayed the video in my head, trying to decipher it. I felt like Luca had told me about his conversion in the hope that I would do the same. But why? Was there any chance, however small, that we would be reunited if I became Muslim? It wasn't entirely implausible...

For the first time in a very long time, a tiny hope glowed in my heart. What did I have to lose? Nothing; I had nothing left, except life and hope.

Thunderstruck

Light flashed through an ebony door,
Its fingers like the stormy glare.
Pure rain flowed like veins, their core
A sky wild with flare.

In my eyes the light gleamed electric,
Bright as a thousand-watt gleam.
Against the darkness it pushed and kicked,
Such an explosion of power I'd never seen.

On forgotten land the lightning glowed
And untamed visions pinned me down.
They crawled around me like shadows
Fallen, dragging the night's ragged gown.

A bolt shot through my belly,
The lightning struck in my eyes
And coursed through my body,
Trapping me in strobing time.

Then lightning ignited under my skin,
Found its way through my bristling hair.
It stoked my heart unbeating,
Chasing shivers everywhere.

Conversion

"*Ashadu an la ilaha illa Allah, Muhammadan rasulu Allah.*"
Amano-Pierre had come over to my spot for no apparent reason. He repeated the same words, looking insistent.

"*Ashadu an la ilaha illa Allah.*"

Clearly he wanted me to repeat, so I tried my hand at Arabic.

"*Asha hadu en lah ilaha in Allah?*"

Amano started to laugh. I knew absolutely nothing about the Arabic language, which has phonemes that are totally foreign to French speakers, sounds that are pronounced with the flat of the tongue and not the tip, or using the roof of the mouth, at the back of the throat, or by breathing in. Amano repeated what he had said, but slowly now, pronouncing each word carefully.

"*Ashadu an la ilaha illa Allah.*"

"*Ashadu an la ilaha illa Allah,*" I said, concentrating.

He smiled at me: I had spoken the words, but they meant nothing to me. Amano went back to the men's camp, proud of himself. He came back the next day, and then the days after, each time adding more words to the prayer.

On the third day, I welcomed him by reciting the full creed.

"*Ashadu an la ilaha illa Allah, wahdahu la sharika la, wa ashhadu anna Muhammadan rasulu Allah.*"

I still didn't know what it meant, but Amano gave me the biggest smile. I couldn't resist, and smiled back at him. I had enjoyed learning something in Arabic—I'd been able to keep my brain busy, and that was priceless. Now I had to find out what the words meant.

I later learned from Luca that I'd recited the Shahada, the profession of faith in Islam. In English, it means *I bear witness that there is no god but Allah, and Mohammed is his prophet.*

By late January 2020, Papadou and Amano-Pierre were more interested in me than ever, visiting me regularly to teach me new Arabic phrases. The last time I had been under the care of Papadou's group was in early December, at the time of my rebellion, and he had only just returned. The atmosphere was completely different now. The Rooster and the second-in-command spoke to me and looked at me with a certain amount of respect. Amano and Papadou were also teaching me Tamasheq, and I, in return, was teaching them French words, which made for some comical moments, since we also have phonemes that are unknown to them. For example, instead of saying *papa*, they say *baba*, because they can't form the sound we associate with the letter *p*. They don't understand how to place their lips. One day I tried to teach Amano-Pierre the correct pronunciation. As he struggled to watch my lip movements, he laughed like a child, hiding his mouth behind his scarf out of modesty as he tried to reproduce the phoneme associated with the *p* in the word *plant*. At one point we were laughing so hard that he was rolling on the ground holding his stomach.

Papadou's group and I had learned to live together and to respect each other. I could have hated them for putting me through such atrocities, for separating me from Luca, for holding my friends—Elisabeth and the others—hostage. But what good would it have done me to darken my heart with hatred? I barely had the courage to survive from day to day, and I would only have made things worse by cursing those men. They didn't know any better;

they had no education. All they seemed to know was the doctrine of the Quran, which they followed to the letter, as well as the commands of their leaders. I was fortunate: some hostages had been tortured and raped under the pretext that they were war booty. But the men who held me did nothing of the kind. They did discipline hostages who caused them problems, and some mujahideen were more rigid than others—Barbarossa and Dentone had sometimes acted erratically—but in general these men didn't resort to gratuitous torture. I had never hated anyone in my life; it's not in my nature, and I certainly wasn't going to start drifting down the grim river of bitterness and animosity. Of course, my benevolence applies to the underlings, the followers, my guards. I don't know if I would have thought so kindly of powerful warlords like Iyad Ag Ghaly, the leader of Nusrat al-Islam, or Amadou Koufa, the Fula leader, who are well aware of the harm they are causing.

Still, I wondered about the men's sudden interest in me. Were they up to something? If not, why were they suddenly treating me differently? The night I had memorized the Shahada, the men rejoiced. It was strange to see them so happy to hear me saying words that made no sense to me. Learning Tamasheq, however, was useful because I could finally express myself and communicate better with the men. We often talked about the stars and the moon when I went to bed by their side after the sun had gone down. I tried to explain to them that the light shining brightly in the sky was not a star, but the planet Venus. Amano told me that he understood, but I think the others were skeptical. The Quran teaches that the sun orbits Earth; that was what the men had learned. Papadou was trying to understand where Canada was. How far was my country from his? The discussion was complex. One day, Papadou asked what we ate in Canada: another difficult explanation. I talked about rice, figuring it must have been familiar because we'd eaten rice with the Arabs in the desert. Yes, he exclaimed, he knew about rice! Those conversations made me feel a little less alone and did my heart good. By then, and as counter-intuitive as it may seem, talking with my captors was solace for my tired mind.

SOME TIME LATER, we moved camp, and a week after that, one afternoon, a motorbike arrived. I had been put up under a towering acacia tree covered with a multitude of fragrant yellow flowers. Little yellow clumps fell from the branches, lining the ground under my gigantic thorny tree. My home smelled delicious, like sweet butter cookies. Sadly, we didn't stay for long, packing up two weeks later. We must not have been hidden well enough.

The man on the motorbike arrived at four. He led the prayer, which was a sign that he was higher up in their hierarchy than Papadou. Since mujahideen never go anywhere for nothing, I had the feeling that he had come to see me, and that his visit had something to do with the Arabic phrases I had been learning for some time now.

After the prayer, Papadou asked me to come to the men's camp, which was unusual. The only time I was allowed to go over—required, actually—was after sunset, to spend the night there under supervision. The stranger motioned for me to sit down on the mat they had put there for me. He stood up and showed me some Arabic phrases on his phone, but I didn't understand, obviously. He chanted the Al-Fātiḥah, the opening surah of the Quran recited at the beginning of every prayer. Every Muslim knows it by heart. As he chanted, he moved his finger from right to left on the screen so that I could follow the Arabic words as he spoke them. Did he know that we didn't share the same alphabet?

Shortly afterwards, as he was speaking to me in Arabic, I picked up the words *chief* and *video* and concluded that he had been sent by Crazy Eyes to convert me. He made it clear that the next day I should purify my body, wash my clothes, and pray. During his visit in December, Crazy Eyes had given me a jilbab, a long, hooded garment worn by women, in a beautiful plum color. I didn't exactly understand what I would use it for. It seemed to me that it would hide me less well, and it would unambiguously reveal my identity as a woman. Now I understood better: I would have to put it on for my conversion. As Luca would have said, *Mamma mia!* What a mess! What was I going to do?

The next day I did everything right: I washed and put on the jilbab. I had also been taught how to perform wudu, which consists of purifying certain parts of the body in a particular order. I had learned the prayers. A prayer has several prescribed steps, and the rules governing it must be followed precisely. I hadn't mastered the teachings on the first try, far from it, but I did my best to imitate the gestures of the men before me. My mentor was satisfied, and left later that day.

From that day on, my life changed. I was now busy with several tasks: I tried to learn the Al-Fātiḥah by heart and I did the five daily prayers behind the mujahideen. I also continued to learn Tamasheq, and Papadou showed me how to become a good Muslim.

A few days after my conversion, the Rooster left the camp one morning on his motorbike and later that day returned with a sheep tied across his legs. The men were euphoric; it was a celebration! One of them tended the fire while another one slit the sheep's throat, cut it into quarters, and hung the meat in a tree to dry in the open air, which would ensure its preservation. That evening there would be a feast. I thought that the men would probably bring me pieces of liver, perhaps ribs or a piece of stomach. What I didn't know yet was that the feast was in my honor, to celebrate my entry into Islam.

The smell of meat roasting on the fire was already wafting over to my tree and mingling with the scent of the flowering acacia. Suddenly, amid the laughter of the men, I heard Papadou shout, *Didi!* He couldn't pronounce Edith, so that was what he called me. He invited me to come with my bowl to the men's camp. I obeyed, wondering what was going to happen to me next. The sun had just set and I could barely make out the men's turbaned faces and their hands as they toiled, intermittently lit by the flickering flames.

Papadou signaled to me that I should sit on the ground and wait. I watched carefully as Amano and the Rooster turned the pieces of meat on the fire and Papadou carved cuts I couldn't identify. I took the opportunity to learn some new Tamasheq words. I pointed to a lung, the heart, the liver, and Amano-Pierre was happy to tell me the names of the organs in his language. When I pointed to a piece Papadou was cutting, Amano started giggling.

"*Aháles!*" In Tamasheq, *aháles* means man.

I turned my gaze to Papadou, who was now placing pieces of "man" in my bowl while scolding Amano for his joke. My eyes were fixed on the piece of mutton, and I couldn't bring myself to put it in my mouth. Meanwhile, Papadou was filling my bowl. Liver, lung, fat fried casings, cubes of meat seared on the coals. I tried to tell him that it was enough, that I couldn't eat all that. I had a small appetite, and I still wasn't much of a meat eater. In the end, though, there was nothing left in my bowl but the fried fat.

It was unusual to share a meal around the fire with the men, and I felt uncomfortable. I didn't like the hypocrisy of the ritual. A week before, I had been worthless, and suddenly I had become their sister because that's what it says in the Quran. Now I was alive, and worthy in the eyes of God. I would have preferred to go back to my blooming acacia tree, but I didn't want to disrespect them or bring myself further misfortune.

I HAD EVERYTHING to learn about Islam. Papadou had given me a book, a bilingual guide to being a good Muslim. He read the rules in Arabic while I followed the French translation on the next page. I never thought that one day I would get caught up in such a whirlwind, but at least my mind was finally focused on something, and that was worth the world. And, deep down, I hoped that my conversion would bring me back to Luca.

One day, before the men had separated us, I had told Luca that I wouldn't convert to Islam, out of respect for Muslims themselves. I didn't want to lie, and make a mockery of their religion. All in all, however, I don't regret my choice. I had to survive, and conversion was the lesser evil. Today, I have kept nothing of their religion, and little by little I forgot even Tamasheq and the prayers. The day we escaped from the mujahideen, I wanted to leave everything behind.

Falling

OCTOBER 2, 2019
289th day in captivity

I fall, fall back,
Fall slant, I fall and curl.
I roll through the air going black,
In the lacy threads of light I whirl.

Like a reflection through the skyscrapered city—
You can see I've injured my wings.
I tumble into the depths of the sea
And plummet to hell, I sink.

I ache and founder to agony,
Scuttled to the pit of the earth
Where the souls of the damned call out to me,
In eternal fire wailing their hurt.

I rise, rise up through the ground.
I climb, climb to the summit,
Clinging to what roots I have found.
Through the earth I push up, a lone violet.

[35]

Race Against
the Setting Sun

ON FEBRUARY 5, I woke before dawn to the sound of the Rooster's voice chanting the adhan, the call to prayer. I had an unexpected feeling of happiness, a lightness in my heart. I couldn't understand why I felt so good. There was nothing special about that day; I would spend it lying on my mat waiting for the next prayer, as I had been doing every day for a week. I would take some time to go over the new Tamasheq words I had learned in my head. I had to find a way to use them during the day so I wouldn't forget them.

I had to get up and perform the ritual cleansing before going to pray with the men. It was a day like any other, yet I felt as happy as a child on Christmas morning.

Before I converted to Islam, I had already been doing sun salutations, a sequence of physical and spiritual postures practiced in yoga. Now I had replaced the sun salutation with a salutation to God. For me, it remained a way of expressing gratitude for Life, and as ever Life responded by blushing the sky and daubing the landscape with rich, warm hues.

Once the morning prayer was over, I rolled up my blanket to head back to my part of the camp—the woman's quarter. I wanted to make a small fire to warm myself until the sun had risen completely. In February the nights were still cold, and there was a significant spread between daytime and nighttime temperatures.

Later that morning, I noticed that the chief and the second-in-command were wearing new clothes. When Papadou passed by my tree, I called out to him.

"*Ihúsken!*" I said—beautiful. He was wearing a royal-blue outfit with gold threads, a departure from his usual sand-colored clothes. The second-in-command, having heard me complimenting his boss, came over to me and strutted around in his new steel-blue garment.

"Hey, you too, *ihúsken!*"

Usually the men always wore the same dull, worn-out clothes; it was nice to see something different, something bright. It put me in a good mood.

That evening, after prayers, the sun was about to set when I heard the sound of a motorbike. Amano, who had left in the morning for some reason, was returning to the camp. Shortly afterwards, Papadou came running over and told me to put all my things in a bag because it was time to leave: *la sortie!* The exit? What? I was getting out? Leaving for real? What about Luca? I couldn't leave without Luca!

Papadou was in a hurry and, seeing that I wasn't moving, he started to stuff my things in a bag himself. Quickly! I had to be quick! The next thing I knew we were running to the motorbike. Amano motioned for me to hop on behind him, and Papadou waved.

Goodbye!

I was alone with the young man on his motorbike, racing against the setting sun. Amano-Pierre wanted to reach our destination before nightfall. Where were we going? I had no idea.

Scene

DECEMBER 8, 2019
356th day in captivity

Running through the midnight streets
In an old black and white,
She stumbles past gray people who flee,
Staring—a shaft of light.

What is it she cradles?
What is her distress?
Through clenched fingers trickle
The colors she wants to possess.

She runs, runs through the crowd
And splatters an old man crimson.
Red pools on the road like a fallen shroud
Staining shoes as she runs and runs.

She dared to steal the setting sun
And leave shooting stars in her wake.
She wrenched the sky and horizon
And stilled them in her gaze.

She shouldn't have stolen from life;
Now she runs and cannot rest.
The universe collapses in the night,
Beauty lost in darkness.

PART VIII

Suleiman and Asiya

In Dreamland

JULY 28, 2019
223rd day in captivity

I've returned from a country that doesn't exist
With dreams on every flower.
Every step I took they sprouted, unasked,
Until I found myself in a tower.

I waited in a time that didn't exist,
Where the present lives once an hour.
From the window, I saw a man in the mist
Plucking armfuls of peaceful colors.

I am the prince of an illusory kingdom,
He said, *dear lady, forgive my slow pace.*
I saw you up there, and I had to come—
You've erred, you don't exist in this place.

You are lost in the stillness of time,
In my country you do not belong.
For you I have picked these blooms in their prime.
Take the sprig and go, move along—

Between dreams and reality you shall find
The path that will bring you back to life.

I turned my gaze to the endless day,
Held my hem and came down from the tower.
I greeted the prince and took the bouquet
And put on the shoes to take every detour.

191

[36]

Suleiman

As we sped off into the sunset, I wondered what exactly Papadou had meant. Did he understand the scope of the word *sortie*? Did he even know what he was saying? He didn't speak French; where had he heard that word? From whose mouth?

Eventually we stopped somewhere in the rocky desert. Amano-Pierre turned to me and signaled that the ride was over, that I should get off the bike. From behind a monolith, a tall, paunchy man came toward us. He greeted Amano, who left right away. In perfect French, the man ordered me to sit in front of the big black rock and wait for him to come back.

He walked away, and I finally lost sight of him behind a huddle of stones. I thought his car must be hidden there. It looked as if these monumental stones had simply plummeted from the sky, landing in the middle of nowhere. The landscape was incredible.

"Hey there... Those clothes look familiar!" a young man exclaimed, walking toward me. "How are you, *principessa*?"

That voice! I couldn't say a word. My breath caught in my throat, and my heart started racing. Luca leaned over to me and gave me the most beautiful smile in the world.

"Hello! You're still wearing the old sweatshirt I lent you. I'm glad to see it's useful!"

"Luca?" I stammered.

His name was the first word that spilled from my lips. I jumped into his arms, and bombarded him with questions.

"How are you doing? Are you feeling well? What are you doing here? I was cold on the bike so I put your sweatshirt on. I always kept it with me and took care of it, it was the only thing I had of yours..."

He smiled at me, obviously as happy as I was that we were together again.

"I'll be right back, I have to go and pray with the men. They're waiting for me over there. Have you converted too? That's what they told me this morning. So now you have to pray too, but alone, because you're a woman. I'll come and get you afterwards. We have a lot to talk about. I'm so happy to see you again! It's a long way back, the camp is six hours from here, to the south. I live there with two other hostages. You're coming with me! When I was told the news this morning, I did a happy dance in front of all the mujahideen! I danced for a long time."

He laughed, told me again that he would come back right after the prayer, and then walked away. For the first time, I prayed alone. With Papadou and his men, I had been learning, so I was allowed to pray with them; they had been my mentors, in a way.

After the prayer, Luca came back.

"Come on, Edith, we're going. We also have to find you a new Muslim name. For them, my name is now Suleiman."

[37]

The Road

WE HAD TO TRAVEL several hundred miles to reach Luca's camp. The journey was long, especially because the drivers stayed off the main roads, taking detours through the mountains to avoid populated areas. I was amazed to hear Luca speak Arabic so well with the driver. He's always had a gift for languages. In addition to his native Italian, he's fluent in Spanish and French, and his English is pretty good. And he had plenty of time to practice the language, particularly because, as a man, he was always with the guards. Because of our genders, he and I had had different experiences.

I was so happy to have my Luca back! I couldn't stop looking at him, listening to him. I wanted him to tell me everything: his journey, his adventures, his misadventures, and to understand how he had managed to hold on, to keep his spirits up, to keep up hope.

He started asking me questions first, about my health, my morale, the last eleven months, but I quickly took over.

"I want to hear what happened on March fourth. Did you know that I wouldn't be getting out?"

"*Mamma mia!*" he said, hiding his face in his hands.

He raised his head, and brushed my cheek with his fingers.

"When I realized that they were splitting us up, I was so enraged that I threw a huge fit, and to punish me they woke me up in the middle of the night and made me walk until I was dead on my feet."

I frowned.

"They made you walk? How far? With whom?"

He went on with his story, gesticulating as only an Italian can. The familiarity of all his little mannerisms was such a pleasure.

"I left with Eyeglasses and Dentone. I didn't have shoes or a sweater, and it was cold that night. The other two had coats on. We walked to a well and came back around noon the next day. I actually collapsed when we got there, I was so tired."

I listened to his story in amazement. The day we had parted, I was so weak from hunger and thirst that I couldn't even lift my blanket. Meanwhile, he'd walked barefoot and freezing across the desert for hours.

"But why would they do that to you? Wasn't it enough to separate us? Those bullies!"

The kidnappers treated men and women differently. I was never punished as severely as Luca, because the men were a little gentler with women, as long as the women stayed submissive. Apart from my short-lived rebellion, I didn't tempt fate by pushing back, and they never laid a hand on me, apart from Barbarossa, who hit me with a stick one night. As my husband, Luca would have been considered responsible for my behavior too, and Barbarossa probably had it in for both of us.

"I think they were afraid I would do something stupid during the night," Luca said. "They didn't trust me. The next day, a stranger came to pick me up and I left the Barbarossa group. I spent ten days with that man, the organization's doctor. He has a prosthetic leg."

"Yes, I met him too. Elisabeth told me that he's not a real doctor. He has some medical knowledge, but he's not a doctor."

"Who's Elisabeth?"

"I'll tell you about it later. I was placed with three women after we were split up..."

I had one burning question on my mind.

"But you . . . Did you try to escape?"

Luca smiled at me, and discreetly put a hand on mine.

"I tried, yes, once, but they caught up with me the next day."

I stared at him, eager to hear the rest of the story.

"Go on! Did you go alone? You told me that you're living with two other hostages. Did they try to escape too?"

"They didn't want to come with me, so I left without them, after dark. My plan was to walk south in the hope of getting to the Niger River after a few days. The problem was that I was too loaded down."

"What had you brought?"

"Packets of dates and two gallons of water, but it was heavy, and grueling."

"You had dates!"

"Yes, you'll see, we have dates. We can eat some tomorrow morning."

Luca was smiling at me. He looked so handsome. As I gazed at him, other questions were running through my head.

"Did you get very far before they caught you?"

"I had covered about twenty miles, I think. But at one point I crossed a sandy area, and that's what gave me away. Turquino, one of the mujahideen, spotted my tracks and followed them. If it hadn't been for that damn Turquino, I might have made it . . . Or I would have died of exhaustion and thirst in the middle of the desert. But, well, he found me. He's clever, that boy. Young, but cunning."

"Where were you when he found you?"

"I was sheltering from the sun behind a stone, resting to regain my strength. Suddenly, in the middle of the morning, I heard motorbikes in the distance. I wasn't well hidden, so I tried to find a better spot, but soon after I heard a walkie-talkie. I was screwed."

I was so caught up in his story that I could sense how devastated he must have been when he was caught.

"Was it Turquino?"

"Yes! Goddamn Turquino! He looked pissed. I tried to escape from him until the very last second, we were running in a circle around the stone."

"Ha! What did he do?"

"He finally pointed his gun at me and it went *click-click*. I realized he wasn't joking and I lay down on the ground."

Luca looked pensive as he watched the road ahead of us fade into the monotonous horizon.

"What happened next? Did they beat you with a pipe and tie you up?"

That was what had happened to poor Mirage. She'd tried to escape twice. The men had beaten her with a piece of pipe and chained her up for several weeks as punishment. It had happened before I arrived; the other two women had told me the story.

"Four or five motorbikes pulled up. The men took me back to the camp, and then, well... They really had it in for me."

I wasn't sure I wanted to hear more, but Luca went on.

"They beat me with a pipe, yeah, and tied me to a tree, under the sun, without a scarf, for a few days."

"Did you even have water?"

"I would ask them for some when I was thirsty, and sometimes they gave me a drink, but not often."

He gave me a loaded glance, and I understood how much he must have suffered from thirst. It was my turn to clasp his hand.

"What happened next? Did they untie you?"

"Yes, but I had chains on my ankles for two months, day and night. Now they only chain me at night."

"When did you try to escape?"

"In September. I converted to Islam in November. The men calmed down a lot after that. Now they invite me to drink tea with them around the fire. I go so I can practice my Arabic. You have to find things to do here, otherwise you lose your mind. The men gave me a bilingual Quran, Arabic–French. I've already read it twice. I'm also learning how to write, thanks to a hostage who knows Arabic well."

We talked for a long time, about religion, about life, about our dreams of freedom. I don't think there was a single moment of silence during the whole six-hour drive. We were rediscovering each other. We had both changed. No one can go through something like this without being changed.

I hadn't seen Luca for eleven months.

Eleven months of suffering. Eleven months of challenges. Eleven months of reflection.

Forest of the Lost

JULY 17, 2019
212th day in captivity

There's something that lingers
In the fog I'm wandering
Between the ferns' green fingers
And the silver sails I'm fumbling.

Here is the breeze, fresh and new,
In my tangled locks
It wisps and weaves through the motionless dew
That blankets this forest of the lost.

Strange words surround me—
I must unravel their meaning.
From the portal of mystery
Our secrets are escaping.

Life has called—
At last I've been found.
It blows on my deserted soul
And heals the festering wound.

Husband and Wife

"WE'LL HAVE TO find you a new name," Luca told me as I got out of the pickup truck.

The moon was already high in the sky, bathing the landscape in a blue glow. Since I had been living only in the natural light of day and night, I had learned to read the cycle of the moon. Judging by its position, it must have been one o'clock in the morning. Unlike us in the West, who use a solar calendar, the Tuareg go by a lunar calendar.

It had been a long drive and we were tired. I was no longer used to a life with so much activity, so much emotion.

"Come on!" said Luca, lifting my bag out of the truck. "There's a big tree over there; it'll be quiet. I used to sleep with the other two hostages and the mujahideen, but now that you're here we have to stay away because the other men aren't allowed to be around my wife. That's what their religion dictates, and they follow it to the letter. You won't even be able to see the other two hostages unless you're veiled. Tomorrow we can build a shelter if you want, but for now let's go to sleep, it's late."

"Good idea," I said, smiling and anticipating the pleasure of finally sleeping in the warmth and safety of Luca's arms. A care-free night of rest, nestled in the warmth of someone I loved. My life would be better with Suleiman by my side.

We played the roles of husband and wife. In Islam, you're only allowed to live with your husband, your family. Among other rules, I had to cover myself completely in the presence of others. At least I now had a shelter, and at home I could take off my headscarf, which I did with great pleasure. The men never saw my face, but Luca told me that they were curious. They asked him about the color of my hair, how long it was, what color my eyes were. He told them I was beautiful; hearing that made me glow. They all had to make up their own image of me, but only Suleiman was allowed to see me, only Suleiman knew me, only he knew who I really was.

There was some interaction between the other two hostages and me through Luca. He was the messenger, passing on questions and answers from one group to the other. Luca told me the story of the two men, and it touched me deeply. I became attached to them from a distance. I would have been so grateful if we had all been able to talk together, face to face, but it was impossible.

From the moment I arrived, my husband took care of me as best he could. He was a master at making bread; he baked it in a small oven he had built himself. He would put a large stone in the fire, then lay it on the coals. He would place the bread on the stone and cover it with an aluminum bowl, and arrange coals in the sand around the bowl, eventually covering it to create an oven. Sometimes he also baked bread in the sand, like the Tuareg. Each technique produced a different type of bread—one was puffier and had a light crumb, while the other, baked in the sand, was more compact and heavier, perfect for taguella.

Every morning Luca offered to make me bread or rice to go with my tea. Truly, the man was a balm for my frazzled spirit. Though I was thin and weak, I was sure that with his care and affection, I would soon be myself again.

One day, after returning from the men's prayer, Luca listed some female Muslim names. I had to pick one.

"Aisha, Fatima, Maryam, Asiya, Laila..."

"I like Asiya. Do you like Suleiman and Asiya?"

"Yes," he answered simply.

We settled into a routine. Luca would fetch wood for the fire, while I gathered acacia flowers to perfume our home with that comforting smell of butter cookies.

One day Luca came back dragging a dead tree. I asked him how he was planning to cut it. Not too surprisingly, since I knew how resourceful he was, I learned that he had already figured it out. He balanced the tree on two stones, one at each end, then lifted a third, heavy stone over his head and threw it with all his might into the middle of the tree. *Crack!* The trunk split into two halves on impact.

"Want to try?" he asked me. He knew I'd get a kick out of it. I always liked to show off my strength.

He placed some branches horizontally on two rocks, then I lifted the rock and managed to throw it against those branches, letting loose a little Amazon yelp. We had a good laugh! I was striking sumo wrestling poses, showing off my Herculean strength before smashing the branches with the stone. At one point, there was only a part of the trunk left; my stone was just bouncing off the wood without cracking it, so I let Luca break off the last pieces. Despite my strength, my husband was much stronger. Still, it felt good to let go a little, to expend some physical energy.

Luca and I stayed positive, as much as possible, to avoid falling into despair. Each of us was careful not to drag the other down with negative thoughts. We were a good team.

Mask of Glass

APRIL 7, 2019
111th day in captivity

She was going in circles across the sand,
She had no name, no hope in her eyes,
No lodestar to light the land
Until she found his soft, inky gaze.

He watched as she made her way
Counting the vultures as she walked past.
She mirrored the desert's every flame
And strode before him in a mask of glass.

Slowly she came near his curious mien,
Trying out every path to her destiny.
But her mask slipped off, shattering
When he took her in his arms, gratefully.

PART IX

The Escape

CAPTIVITY: DAY 451 TO FREEDOM: DAY 1

Upside Down

SEPTEMBER 21, 2019
278th day in captivity

The wind is my skipper,
It flips me upside down.
Find your star, it whispers.
But it's the universe I found.

In the Milky Way I float along,
Nebulae daub me with white
And guide me to where constellations sing
In a starry garden of light.

I pluck the life that waits for me,
Blooming through pinpricks
In velvet infinity,
Cloaked in colors exotic.

I skim the scent of the wind
And find at last my wandering ship.
I follow an exquisite music tinged
With the waves' every crest and dip.

The earth is topsy turvy,
It spins in the sky's surging whims.
Ephemeral time falters, dizzy.
Seen and unseen are reversed in the wind.

continued overleaf

On the sea a gale is rising,
The surge against my wooden barque—
The roiling sea looms, pulsing
As I leave behind the unfolding dark.

I sail to the edge of night
And close my eyes a minute,
Dreaming of a brand-new life
Shaped by the wind that brought me to it.

[39]

Planning

SINCE I'D ARRIVED at the camp, the guards no longer chained
Luca at night. Perhaps they thought he wouldn't try to escape
now that he had his wife with him, or maybe they figured that six
months in chains was punishment enough. As far as I know, no
one had ever managed to escape—no one could escape the desert,
the vast, arid sweep that was our cage. Mirage had tried twice, but
the men had found her quickly, hidden under a solitary tree, lost
in the middle of the sand.

The guards also relaxed a bit because Luca and I had converted
to Islam. According to the Quran, we were now their brother and
sister, and they had to treat us with respect, even though they were
holding us hostage. The only thing Luca still had to do was to bring
them our shoes at sunset; he got them back every morning. Also,
we were given our water ration at the beginning of the day, so that
by evening we were almost out. Perhaps they thought that without
water or shoes we wouldn't dare run away across that land gashed
with razor-sharp stones.

But in spite of these restrictions, a plan began to form in our minds.

"At one point," Luca told me one day, "when we were going to
get you in the north, just before the meeting place, I saw a truck
passing in the distance."

He had my full attention.

"Go on."

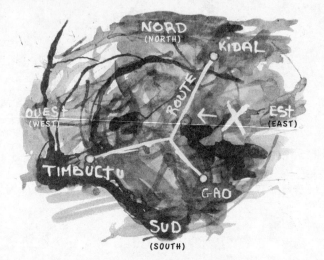

Luca took up a stick and traced a map of Mali in the sand. Then he drew a triangle, with Kidal, Timbuktu, and Gao at each point.

"According to the calculations I drew up with the other two hostages, we should be near this triangular area."

He marked our presumed position, just east of the triangle, with an X.

"The truck I saw must have been driving on the main road to Kidal."

He drew a line—a beautiful line!—along the north–south axis, to the left of the X.

"So if we were to go west, we should cross that road. The problem is I don't know how far away it is. It could be twenty miles away, or thirty or sixty miles away."

I was impressed. How could he know all that? Of course, I had already noticed his ability to calculate everything—how many miles we'd traveled, our orientation, everything. He had excellent observation skills, and a good memory. But Mali is immense, and as far as I was concerned we could have been anywhere. I just had to trust Luca and the other two hostages. It was our only chance. I nodded in agreement.

"The moon will be full in a week and a half," I said. "That night it will rise at sunset, but after that it will come up a little later each night. After three or four days, we should have a few hours of darkness to escape."

"Okay, good idea. And we can orient ourselves by Venus at the beginning of the night, before the moon rises."

"Do you think the other two will come with us?"

"They told me once that they would never try to escape. So it's better to keep this to ourselves. It's more discreet, and it won't get them into trouble if we do make it."

I could feel a sense of hope returning to me. The likelihood of escape might be small, but I was willing to take that chance. I had no desire to live with armed men for the rest of my life.

"I have a second pair of shoes they don't know about," I told Luca. "They didn't search my bag when I arrived. I could sew you some shoes with the fabric from my mat, which is stiff enough, and make some cardboard soles. Do you think you could find a needle for me?"

He nodded.

"We have a gallon jug," he added. "Between now and the night we leave, we have time to save enough water from our rations and showers to fill it."

I was thrilled.

"Are you sure, Edith, that you're prepared to take the risk? You know, if the other two hostages refuse to flee, it's because the chances are eight out of ten the men are going to catch us, one out of ten we'll die of thirst, and there's a one in ten chance that we'll succeed. It's not much, you know."

I told myself that one chance in ten was not nothing: it was the possibility of freedom.

"Let's get ready." I was determined. "And if the circumstances are good, we'll leave."

"We can't leave any traces in the sand, otherwise they'll find us for sure. That's what happened to me last time."

"I'll wrap my shoes in fabric to reduce our tracks. You could also plant false trails before we leave. We have to gain as much time as we can—the success of our plan depends on it."

For once, time was on our side.

Mystery

I saw you in the yonder
Passing through mysteries.
The haze around every wonder
In your wake, in your gaze the key.

Why do you wear that impish smile?
Why do you muddle forth?
Now twilight becomes an eagle
That's caught me in its sights.

Symbols take shape beneath you
And swirl quietly in the air.
Their reflections gild the dew
And turn to the top of elsewhere.

Your lips move wordlessly
As I watch your stride, long and wide.
I know you've watched me secretly;
I've seen your smiling eyes.

[40]

Preparations

TWO NIGHTS AFTER the full moon, Luca gently woke me from sleep. When I opened my eyes, he was leaning over me.

"What's going on?"

"Listen to that wind... It's blowing so hard that it would definitely erase our tracks if we ran away tonight!"

I straightened up on one elbow to look outside. A sand wind! It was rare for sand winds to blow at night. When they did, they tended to last either one night or three nights in a row. The desert has its little rituals too.

I sat up.

"What time do you think it is?"

"I don't know, my watch isn't working, but according to the moon it must be about one o'clock in the morning."

"We don't have enough time, Luca. The men get up at half past four for the dawn prayer, they'll notice right away that you're not there."

Luca hesitated. He wanted to take advantage of the wind, but he knew that I was right. I had a different idea.

"Tonight is too late, we're not ready. But if it's a three-night wind, we could leave tomorrow, after the last evening prayer. And it'll be dark for longer before the moon rises. What do you think?"

Luca had calmed down a bit from his excitement over the wind.

"Okay," he said. "Let's hope the wind picks up again tomorrow night. Go back to sleep. Good night."

He lay down, watching the sand whip around.

"I hope there will be wind tomorrow night too," he said. "Tonight the whole desert will be swept away. By tomorrow morning, we won't see any trace..."

He looked shaken, uncertain. Conflicting emotions played across his eyes. I snuggled up to him. It was windy. It was cold.

DAWN.

The call to prayer rose up into the morning. The first light of day was just spreading across the sky. We got up to perform wudu, and Luca went to join the men as I was about to do my solo prayer outside our shelter. I had to bow eastward, toward the shrine of the Kaaba—the holiest place in Islam, in Mecca. Luca had learned Arabic and read the Quran, so he had taught me all this and more.

As soon as the prayer was over, I crawled back between my sheets to warm up. I heard Luca's footsteps coming back.

"Would you like me to bake you some bread?" he asked me, though he already knew my answer.

"Yes, thank you, you're sweet!" I replied with a smile, tucked under the sheets.

The day passed slowly. We had managed to accumulate enough water to escape. If we rationed ourselves as much as possible, we might have enough for two or three days. I had made two small backpacks out of one of my jackets so that we could carry the water and some dates. I had also sewn Luca a pair of shoes, which seemed reasonably sturdy and almost comfortable, and a small belt bag into which I would tuck my poems. (I thought often of Elisabeth, who had encouraged me to write a book of poetry.) Luca also wanted to keep some of his writings, so I added them to mine. If the men caught up with us, we risked losing the documents forever, so I would wear the bag around my waist, hidden under my clothes.

After the afternoon prayer, Luca returned, visibly worried:

"All the footprints have been erased by last night's wind. If we leave tonight and there's no wind, there will be only our tracks in the sand. The men will find us easily."

He was right, but I wanted to be encouraging.

"Let's be confident. We can use the time we have left to deceive the men. Can you take off your shoes and make footprints in the sand in the opposite direction to the one we'll be heading?"

"I'll try after the sunset prayer, but I can't promise anything."

It was risky, since the guards could catch him in the act. And he would have to come back to our shelter without leaving any trace of his return, a tricky thing indeed.

The hours dragged on interminably as we waited for the sun to set. I took the opportunity to finalize the details. We had to play our cards right; there was no room for error. During our escape, every second would count.

To make the men think I was sleeping, I stuffed sand into a pair of pink pants I usually wore to bed and placed them under the blanket, and shaped a female body with bags. I was proud of my work: it was pretty realistic. The knee of a bent leg even peeked out a little from under the blankets. I arranged Luca's blankets to make the men think he had gotten up.

My plan was simple: when they noticed Suleiman's absence at prayer, the men would come and look in the shelter. Seeing that his wife was still in bed, they wouldn't worry, perhaps thinking that he had simply gone to the toilet, giving us a few precious extra minutes. The men wouldn't dare to wake a woman, at least not until they suspected one of their hostages had escaped.

When Luca saw my setup, he froze, as if he'd been struck by lightning. He was quiet for a few seconds.

"If they catch up with us, we're dead."

I burst out laughing, even though it wasn't funny at all. It was certain that the mujahideen wouldn't be amused by our deception. I was putting everything on the line. We had to make it.

The wind, our ally at night, could also weaken us: it was cold. I had an idea—I cut two ponchos out of the large square of plastic I had been given during the rainy season. I hoped that they would help protect us from the wind.

"It's time for the last prayer," Luca told me.

He still seemed undecided. I knew he was worried about me; my health wasn't great. I still hadn't recovered my strength after my second hunger strike. I had worms, cramps, and abnormal bleeding. The cold nights and the wind also exhausted me. Since I had been back with Luca, my condition was improving gradually, but I was still finding it difficult to gather my strength. Luca was afraid I wouldn't be able to keep up with him.

"Good luck, Luca. I'll get everything ready, and we'll leave the first chance we get. The wind seems to be picking up, which is a good sign. Did you manage to plant any false tracks?"

He nodded and left to join the mujahideen.

The wind was blowing harder and harder.

The skies were on our side too.

Night

THE WIND SLIPPED through the branches and thorns of the acacia trees, snatching a few flowers as it went. It spun through the desert and caught my headscarf, making it dance. I was grateful for the powerful wind: not only would it erase the signs of our passage, but it would also muffle the sound of our footsteps on the rocks.

I was ready to leave, waiting for Luca, who was finishing the prayer with the men on the other side of the camp. It was almost pitch black, the sandy wind blurring the sky, dimming the faint glow of the stars. All the conditions were right for our escape: we would be invisible. In fact, it might even have been a little too dark; Luca would have to concentrate to find our way through the darkness.

Our camp was set up on a strip of sand, in a wadi where some greenery grew: trees, shrubs, flowers, tall grass. But only a few yards from our shelter began the immense stretch of rock of the desert zone. Luca and I had named the two zones where we had been held the sand desert and the rock desert. In the first, the sand desert, only acacia trees and some hardy grasses grow among the dunes. Nothing else can survive. That's where we were held captive from January 2019 until mid-August the same year. The second, our main home under the Tuareg, was an inhospitable place almost entirely covered in rock. Yet there were wadis, and it was on these green strips of land that we were held captive by the Tuareg. Luck had brought Luca and me together again in the rocky desert, which would allow us to escape without leaving too obvious a trace. And when we crossed the sand, the wind would erase our steps.

The desert is so vast that it seems infinite, especially when you're thinking of escaping. I stared out into the deep night that stretched before me, hundreds of square miles. The emptiness could have frightened me, but I felt freedom out there—the wind, the spirit of the earth blowing on my hopeful soul. The wind rushed through the desert, through that unfathomable darkness. Freedom was impatient; it was already brushing against my hand and caressing my face, but I had to wait for Luca to come back, for Suleiman to finish his prayer. I knew he was nervous, and I also knew he was worried about my frailty. But he had to trust me. I was tenacious, determined.

Suddenly I felt a presence close to me. Luca.

"Are you ready, dear Asiya?"

"Yes, I'm ready, I was waiting for you."

He went into the shelter, put on his shoes, and layered the plastic poncho under his clothes so that it wouldn't blow noisily in the wind. Then he placed the water jug and the dates in his backpack. He took a deep breath, closed his eyes, opened them again, and looked at me seriously.

"Are you sure you want to go through with this? It's very risky."

He took my hand in his, waiting for my answer.

"Yes, Luca, I'm sure. I'm ready."

At my words, he pulled me forward. Without my contact lenses, I couldn't see anything in the dark. Luca would have to lead me until the moon came out. I followed him cautiously, worried that I might make a false move that would alert the mujahideen, who were chatting around the fire.

Luca led me to the rocks, the first crucial step. We couldn't make any noise, or nudge the tiniest stone. I put one foot on the rocks, then the other. The tension was high; we were close to the men. Luca held my hand firmly, supporting my arm. I was moving slowly, slower than a tired turtle, slower even than time in the desert. Once we were out of earshot of the armed men, I began to breathe again, and we started walking faster. We had to put space and time between us and them as quickly as possible.

Freedom was ahead of us; it was calling to us in the blowing wind. It carried all our hopes, and we were following. To escape, we had to flee through the night, black as our fear, black as the immensity of the universe, black as all the mysteries, black as the doors of destiny. Black as our path. We didn't say a word, we didn't dare make the slightest noise until we had crossed at least the first mile.

As I was going down a small hill, I stepped on a rock that rolled away beneath my foot, and I twisted my knee. I didn't want to panic Luca, so I didn't tell him I had hurt myself.

Shortly afterwards, I broke the silence, asking him in a low voice if he could see anything in the thick night.

"Not really, no," he replied, squeezing my hand, "but I'm heading toward Venus. Can you see it?"

He pointed to the one bright spot in the foggy sky that would guide us for an hour.

"Hopefully the sky will clear a bit so I can see the constellations while we're waiting for the moon. How are you doing? You're walking funny. Are you hurt?"

"I twisted a knee going down the hill, but it's nothing."

"You hurt yourself?" He stopped short.

"Don't worry," I said. "Let's go!"

He let go of my hand and instead took my arm to help me walk without any further missteps.

Suddenly he stopped again.

"Shit, I'm soaked."

"What?"

"The jug is leaking."

He took off his backpack and took out the water jug to assess the damage.

"Have we lost a lot of water?"

"Yes. I think the cap doesn't seal. It's not airtight."

I tore off a piece of my plastic poncho and handed it to him.

"Here, put that over the bottle before you screw the cap back on."

Luca thanked me, put the water can back in his bag, and hung it on his chest, so he could hold the jug with his free arm to prevent it from moving, and hopefully prevent another leak.

After a few miles, I asked him if his shoes were holding up.

"Yeah, they're good. How's your knee?"

"It's okay."

"You're limping, Edith. I can see you're in pain. Here, take a painkiller, I have three."

"Not necessary. I just have to be careful."

I couldn't see where I was stepping on the uneven ground, and my injured knee was twisting all over the place, but I had refused the medicine because I didn't know how long our journey would last. For the time being, the pain was tolerable, and it was better to save the painkillers, especially as Luca was prone to back pain.

Poor Luca had stopped talking; I could feel him worrying. Concentrated on his task, he guided me, while watching over the water can to avoid losing any more of our precious nectar of life.

Venus had just dropped below the horizon, and the moon still hadn't risen. Luca stopped and began scanning the sky.

"Can you see anything?"

"Yes, the sky has cleared up a bit. There's Orion!"

He was looking for constellations to guide him. Yet again, my friend proved brave and resourceful—his strength seemed boundless. I was so glad, so relieved to be with him in the hours when our lives were at stake.

A little later, farther on, Luca told me that we had to cross some mountains.

"Can you see them?" he asked, pointing to the black horizon.

"A little..."

"I think we can pass between those two hills over there to save time, but we have to turn off a bit to the north."

"Okay. How's it going with the jug?"

"It's still leaking," he sighed. "I'm all wet."

He stopped to check the water and sighed again.

"We've lost a lot."

The wind was blowing harder and harder.

"You must be cold, soaking wet like that."

I didn't know how to help him. He closed his eyes for a moment, as if to collect himself, then he stood up, placed the bag back on his chest, and took me by the hand.

"Let's go."

A celestial glow was now lighting up the night behind us: the moon was rising. Something on the ground caught my eye—a piece of cardboard. I showed it to Luca. He bent down with a frown, then his eyes grew wide and he hurried to check his shoes.

"They're tearing on the rocks."

I tore off one of the pieces of fabric I had hung on my bag. I knew they would come in handy.

"Here, wrap this around your shoes, it should protect them a bit."

He took the cloth and tore it in half to wrap his feet. Then he realized that I had seen the piece of cardboard on the ground.

"Hey! Can you see now?"

"Yes, thanks to the moon. Thank you, Luca. Thank you!"

I wanted him to know that I was grateful for everything he did for me. I could never thank him enough.

"Let's keep going," he smiled.

Now that the moon was shining on us, things would be a little easier, and we set off again, but after a few hours of walking west, I had to stop.

"Luca?"

"What's going on, *principessa*?"

"I think I'll take a painkiller now."

His jaw tightened, and I saw that he was growing more concerned.

"You're in pain, Edith! I knew it. Do you want to take a break?"

"No. I just want a painkiller."

He pulled a caplet from his pocket and gave it to me, then took the water jug out of his bag.

"Thank you, Luca."

It did us good to drink a little, but we had lost about a third of our water.

"Do you want to continue right away or take a rest?"

"Let's keep going."

I noticed that the cloth Luca had wrapped around his shoes was trailing behind him in tatters. I gave him another piece of fabric, and while he wrapped his shoes again, I picked up the rags so we didn't leave any clues behind.

"Do your feet hurt?"

"Don't worry about me," he replied, but his voice betrayed fatigue and worry.

He had rolled up so many layers of cloth that his shoes now looked like big slippers. We continued on our way. Luca was moving at a pretty fast pace, while I hobbled along behind. I couldn't bend my knee anymore, it hurt too much.

Suddenly, we came across wheel tracks on the ground! Luca peered at them.

"They're not too wide or hollow. They're not truck tracks. It's probably not the road we're looking for. What do you think?"

"I think you're right, it's probably a small side road used by the mujahideen."

Luca nodded and we resumed walking west. We had to stop several times to repair his shoes, which the sharp rocks were shredding. I was running out of fabric. Every time we stopped, we ate a few dates and drank some water. At one point, during one of these rest stops, Luca stood looking out at the flatness before him, the landscape empty of any plants or stones. He was pensive.

"It might be wise to stop soon. We should spend the day in a good hiding place and hope our captors don't find us. Your knee is too sore, and the night is ending."

"Let's walk at least until sunrise!"

"No," he insisted. "Let's stop."

Luca looked completely defeated. I looked at him, disgruntled.

"Luca, do you want freedom, or do you want chains?"

My words gave him a jolt, and he seemed to gather courage. He got up and took me by the arm to help take weight off my knee. We started walking again toward our freedom. We were heading west, to the main road. It had to be somewhere.

Of Hope and Darkness

Darkness hunted, hobbling through,
It stumbled along in alleys.
It stalked my hopes where they were strewn
And licked its lips at its prey.

Fleeing the noise, I groped along—
I only wanted to find a way out,
I didn't know I'd chosen wrong,
Stumbling on seeping doubt.

The darkness smelled of such purity,
Like delectable hope hard won.
And hope reached out, tempting liberty,
Guiding our steps to freedom.

[42]

Freedom
at Daybreak

WE HAD TRAVELED a considerable distance over the rocky terrain without leaving any tracks. There had been a few sandy areas too, where Luca passed behind me to erase our footprints. The strong wind took care of the rest.

For the past while, a white expanse had been stretching before us as far as the eye could see, melting into the distance. If we had to cross that desolate terrain, it would be impossible not to leave footprints. But we had no choice; we had to keep moving.

Suddenly, Luca called out.

"Look, Edith! A car went by here!"

The fresh tire tracks showed that the vehicle had been heading west through the white desert. We didn't know if they would lead us to the main road to Kidal, but at least they were going in the right direction! I watched my companion walk ahead of me in the providential tracks and felt a strange sense of well-being. I was serene and calm, overwhelmed by the good omens. It was as if freedom had whispered a secret—a sweet, wonderful secret called victory.

Less than an hour later we reached another, much busier road running roughly north–south. Multiple tracks, wide and deep, suggested that trucks traveled on this road. Was it the main road to Kidal? Luca doubted it. We had walked for eight hours, but we couldn't have covered more than twelve miles. Would our captors have held us prisoner so close to the main road?

"What do you think, Edith?"

Did we take the risk of stopping here or should we keep walking? I didn't dare speak, but my intuition, the feeling of impending success, made me believe we had found the main road.

We were thinking about this when we realized that it was nearly five in the morning. We had to hide.

"We should hide close to the road," I said to Luca. "Later, when the sun is up, we'll see if there are a lot of cars and trucks going by."

"Okay, there are some shrubs over there, let's see if they'll do."

We walked about half a mile northwest to find the perfect hiding place: a shrub that would also protect us from the wind.

"Stay close to me," Luca said. "I'll cover us with the turban."

He did his best to warm us up, but we were so cold that, even though we were exhausted, we couldn't sleep without a blanket. I closed my eyes anyway, trying to recover as best I could while we waited for the sun. What was next? Anything could happen. If the mujahideen found us, would they let us live? And if they did spare our lives, how would they punish us? Would they separate us for good? Was this the last time I would get to snuggle with Luca? I hugged him even tighter.

Minutes passed, and I couldn't still my mind. If a truck passed by on the road, would it stop for us? Would they take us? If we saw only cars or pickup trucks, could we trust them? There must have been a lot of rebels in the area. Were we about to walk into an ambush? And if this wasn't the road to Kidal, if we had to keep walking west, how long would our water last? We had lost a lot and drunk little, for fear of running out, but our supply wouldn't last forever.

Suddenly, at around seven in the morning, we heard an engine in the distance. Luca scrambled up.

"The mujahideen?"

Obviously, we had the same fear. I didn't know what to say. How could we tell if they were good guys or bad guys? Luca crouched down by the shrubs, peering at the road in the distance. He still couldn't see anything, and he was so focused that I kept quiet. He seemed ready to pounce, waiting...

"It's a truck! Follow me!" he shouted, taking off like a shot.

I don't think I've ever seen him run so fast! I jumped out of our hiding place, but my knee made me limp. I felt like a pirate with a wooden leg, but at least I was making progress. Far ahead of me, Luca was waving toward the road to get the driver's attention, but the driver either didn't see him or didn't want to stop, and he sped off in front of us, leaving a billowing trail of sand and dust in his wake. Luca stopped to catch his breath, then came back to me.

"We're too far from the road."

He was right. We searched the area for another hiding place and found a bush closer to the road. It would be less concealed from the mujahideen, but we had no choice. We had to hope that some well-meaning driver would pick us up before our captors got hold of us.

An hour later we heard another engine in the distance, coming from the south, and Luca jumped to his feet. Again, the same agonizing question: good guy or bad?

"There are two trucks!" Luca cried. "Let's go!"

And he took off, running as fast as he could—against time, against our captivity, against the shackles that had bound us. What a sprinter he'd turned out to be, I thought as I hobbled along far behind. I could see Luca gesturing in the middle of the road to get the attention of the drivers. The first truck continued without slowing down, a cloud of dust swirling behind it, but the second slowed down... and stopped. I saw Luca climb onto the running board to talk to the driver. When I finally reached them, Luca came to me, and took my bag.

"He says he'll take us, I think. He doesn't speak Arabic very well and it's hard for us to understand each other. He was pretty startled when he saw that I'm white!"

Luca helped me into the cab of the truck, and we sat down on the wide bench seat. I was right up against the passenger door. Our faces were hidden, with only our eyes peeking through the folds, and I wasn't sure if the driver had noticed that I was a woman. I didn't want to speak, lest my voice betray me. I just nodded to the driver and the old man sitting next to him. They looked alike, a father and son, surely. We were sitting comfortably in the truck, so close to freedom, dressed as two white men fleeing their desert jailers. I wondered if the two men had grasped the drama that was playing out before their eyes.

I caught Luca's eye—a look full of hope, certainly, but also concern. What would happen to us now? Luca asked where we were going. Kidal, the driver answered. We crossed our fingers.

But half an hour later, a pickup truck—the same kind the mujahideen drove—started chasing down our truck. We could see in the rearview mirror that a passenger was waving to our driver to stop. Luca and I exchanged a helpless look: our captors had caught up with us.

The truck pulled over to the side of the road, and a mujahid we didn't know came to speak to the driver. His voice was terrifying. I was shaking to the core of my being. He questioned the truck driver, who answered energetically. They seemed to be snickering at something. Until now, our driver had seemed to me like a calm, composed man, which gave me the feeling that now he was playacting. As for the old man, he seemed to understand the seriousness of the situation, and moved forward to hide us. The seconds ticked by, and I hardly dared to breathe, staring at the floor of the cab.

Finally, the mujahid went back to his pickup, and our driver started up again. We were back on our way to Kidal, safe and sound! From then on, I decided to call our driver the Guardian

Angel. I tried to sneak a peek at him to guess what he was feeling. He had grown serious again, as before, but now he seemed worried too. The mujahideen truck turned back, leaving us in the clear.

Our driver must have lied. He had saved our lives. I couldn't believe it. Shortly afterwards, another truck caught up with ours, and both came to a halt at the side of the road. The Guardian Angel and his father got out to talk to the other driver. Watching them gesture in the rearview, I saw that they knew each other. When the men got back into the truck, the older one took my place against the door, pushing me to the middle so he could watch what was going on behind us in the mirror. He kept the driver informed of what he saw. The other truck followed us like a shadow.

During the whole journey, our Guardian Angel veered off the road whenever he saw a vehicle coming in the opposite direction, and the truck would lumber off into the sandy desert, presumably to keep us out of sight of other travelers. The second truck, on the other hand, stayed on the road, driving slowly, waiting for us to return. We drove on like that for hours until we reached a small town.

Kidal, at last!

The Guardian Angel stopped his truck in front of a government building, and the old man waved us out. End of the line.

We were free.

We thanked our brave rescuers warmly over and over. They were leaving us in good hands.

Could it be true? Had we made it? Were we really free? It didn't feel real.

We entered the building, where two men, both French, took us in. They were with MINUSMA, the United Nations Stabilization Mission in Mali, a UN peacekeeping operation. The two men had a lot of questions.

We were free. Was this possible? To be honest, I didn't believe it; I couldn't believe it. We couldn't just be free, just like that, magically! Not after the fifteen months we had just lived through. What about all the others who were still being held prisoner in the desert? What would happen to the other hostages? The mujahideen must have been livid. A million thoughts crashed around in my head.

Everything happened quickly after that. MINUSMA officers gave us food, and we were able to shower. They brought us clean clothes. A doctor examined us and gave me an anti-inflammatory for my knee. Everything was falling into place. The men notified our respective governments. Transport would be organized the next day: a helicopter to Gao, a larger town to the south, then a plane to Bamako, the capital of Mali.

We were free. It was difficult to take in at the time, but freedom was taking shape before us, with all its colors and possibilities. And it was beautiful, more beautiful than it had ever been before.

Guardian Angel

The softest wings swept by me,
Ornate with virtue and light—
A herald of the galaxy
Blinding me as I tumbled from flight.

In the distance an angel had risen,
Shaking his feathers askew,
Knocking down the stars from the heavens
And clinging as they fell or they flew.

His was such strange beauty.
In his eyes shooting stars shone.
He fluttered his pale lashes softly
As he looked upon my sighing soul.

He held the whole sky aloft.
Indigo dust lined his palms.
He sprinkled the stars on my path
And the purest of them beckoned.

Again and again he turned my way,
Smiling at me from afar.
My time was not over, he seemed to say;
Then he spread his wings toward another star.

PART X

Three Countries

FREEDOM: DAY 1 TO DAY 7

[43]

Mali

L UCA WHISPERED IN my ear, stroking my arm, not wanting
to startle me.

"Edith, wake up...It's already four o'clock, we have to get ready
to take the helicopter."

I was lying in a hospital bed in a room at the MINUSMA head-
quarters. We had been able to get some sleep after the French
army's questioning, which had lasted until midnight. France had
been fighting terrorists in Mali since the 2013 rebellions. I was
worn out; we hadn't slept the previous night. My eyelids felt so
heavy, I could barely open my eyes. Suddenly, I remembered: we
were free! That woke me up. This new reality felt barely tangible; I
had a hard time taking it in. I looked up at Luca—this young man,
who was also free—and smiled at him.

"Do you realize that we're free?"

"Yes, we are free," he replied gently. "How do you feel?"

"I feel like...it's hard to believe."

"Me too." He smiled tenderly.

Someone knocked on the door, and Luca went to open it. A man
whose nationality I couldn't tell announced that a car was waiting
for us.

"We'll be there in five minutes," Luca said.

Luca didn't like to keep people waiting, I knew that, so I quickly went to brush my teeth. I was in awe of everything that was being done for us, the mountains that all these people were trying to move. For the past twelve hours, hundreds of human beings had been mobilized around us. I don't know what everyone was doing exactly, but I felt guilty for causing so much trouble. I wanted to curl up in a tiny ball and not bother anyone. I knew I couldn't; that wasn't how things were going to unfold. I would be taken home, no matter what. I would be protected. What a difference a day can make.

Before leaving, we thanked everyone, especially the French man who had taken such good care of us. Before saying goodbye, he handed us a folded blue bundle.

"Take this with you, it can get cold in the helicopter."

"Thank you," I replied quickly, accepting his gift.

I discreetly brushed my cheek against the blanket he'd given me. Finally, something soft, not rough. My life was getting better every second.

Luca held my hand all the way to the helicopter. I wondered how he was feeling. He didn't express his emotions easily, so I often had to try to decipher his body language. We were the first to board with our escort, then the helicopter filled with other civilians who were leaving for Gao, like us.

Near the end of the 170-mile flight, Luca pointed through the window to a small town. We were wearing noise-canceling headsets, so I just nodded in reply. We were reaching our destination.

At the airport in Gao, we were met by a man who took us to the VIP lounge. He offered us food and drink while we waited for our next flight. Shortly afterwards, the man who had escorted us from Kidal boarded a small plane with us for Bamako, the capital. His mission was to hand us over to the Malian authorities, and then Canada would take over, but not right away. We didn't understand much of the diplomatic ballet; we just did what we were told.

When we got off the plane in Bamako, we were caught off guard by cameras, flashbulbs—havoc! *Luca Tacchetto and Edith Blais, two hostages finally found! The Italian and the Canadian had been freed!* Journalists were causing quite a ruckus around us.

"How do you feel after fifteen months in captivity?"

I was in shock, bewildered, jostled. We were led to a building, but before we could enter, a woman wearing a mask took our temperature. At the entrance to the building, an African man came toward us and introduced himself: he was the head of MINUSMA.

"We spoke on the phone last night," he reminded us.

I wanted to shake his hand, but he offered me his elbow instead. Tentatively, I touched his elbow with mine. Some African handshake, perhaps? In any case, it confused me so much that I burst out laughing.

Another man came along, giving us the same elbow shake. I was still laughing. I was amused by what I assumed was an African custom, especially since the man wasn't African; he was the Canadian ambassador to Mali. Luca also seemed to find the gesture comical. The ambassador realized that we didn't know what was going on in the world, so he explained that we were in the middle of a pandemic. For the first time, I heard about the coronavirus. While we were sequestered in the desert, I had so often wondered what was happening elsewhere on the planet.

We met a host of important men and followed them into a room. I turned to the ambassador.

"Could the media please leave the room? I need to breathe."

"Of course!"

He politely asked the journalists to leave. A woman who worked for Global Affairs Canada, the department responsible for diplomatic relations, explained that she and I would talk later.

In that room, we had to answer a battery of questions. I spoke on the phone with the Canadian minister of foreign affairs. He had been in touch with my family since he heard the big news overnight. He couldn't wait to hug me, he said. Several of the officials who had been trying to find me for fifteen months had started crying when they heard that we'd escaped. It moved me deeply to learn that so many strangers cared about our well-being.

"Would you like me to pass on a message to your family?"

"Tell them I'm fine and that I love them!"

He also told me that he had contacted the Italian foreign minister. He wanted to know if Luca and I wanted to stay together for the time being.

"We don't want to separate you. We were thinking of sending you together to a hospital in Germany."

I turned to Luca, who had just gotten off the phone with the Italian foreign minister. Did he want to come with me to Germany? He said yes, the minister had just told him about the idea. So I accepted the Canadian official's proposal. I thought my government was particularly humane and generous to take my Italian friend under its wing like that, in order not to separate us after our traumatic experience.

Throughout my captivity, I had wondered about Canada's involvement in the case. I had wondered if people in high places knew my name, if they were aware of my disappearance, and I was touched by all the expressions of sympathy and humanity. The Canadian minister of foreign affairs told me that he spoke Italian, and that he would like to speak to Luca. I handed my friend the phone.

Afterwards, I answered questions from the head of MINUSMA and another senior official in the Malian government. I was a bit overwhelmed. When the discussions were over, we were told that the president of Mali wanted to meet us. We left the room and plunged back into the media madness. Totally disoriented by all the hubbub, I followed Luca closely, as if I wanted him to protect me. I had become accustomed to silence, to solitude, to the presence of only our shadows. Now, in the noisy crowd, I was lost, and the microphones shoved in my face made me dizzy.

We got into a pickup truck driven by Malian soldiers. Another pickup zigzagged ahead of us through the bustle of Bamako, with machine gun–toting soldiers in the back. Several other vehicles were following us. Our escort was honking madly to warn civilians of our passage. We brushed dangerously close to the cars, passing at full speed. I wondered how the armed men managed to stay upright in the back of the truck. At one point a policeman on a motorcycle moved to the front of the procession, his siren blaring, which at least quelled the honking.

I was worried because I knew that the mujahideen were everywhere, even in Bamako. We weren't moving quietly, and I was afraid we would be easy prey for Al-Qaeda. Maybe the extremists were dreaming of teaching us a lesson, showing the world that no one can escape their clutches. I imagined them watching for us, armed with rocket launchers. The behavior of the Malian military was incomprehensible. Luca too looked baffled. He seemed shaken.

"We'll have survived this, too!"

Luca squeezed my hand to reassure me.

At one point, a woman driving in the nearby traffic lost control of her motorbike, probably thrown off by our cacophonous convoy. I saw the poor woman crash to the ground. Passersby ran to help, but we continued on our way as if nothing had happened.

"Stop!" I shouted, pointing at the accident victim.

Luca turned around.

"*O cazzo!*" he swore.

Later, the doctor who looked after me until I returned to Canada told me that, that day in Bamako, Canadian soldiers were following us until Mali had officially handed us over to Canada. Politics, protocol, diplomacy—nevertheless, they were there, keeping us safe in the midst of the chaos. The bald, burly doctor, whom I called Mr. Clean, told me that he had seen the woman fall off her motorbike too. He had immediately asked the driver to stop, but they couldn't disobey the orders they had to follow us. So no one stopped to help the woman. What an odd, frightening situation.

We finally arrived at our destination, the presidential residence looming up ahead. Journalists chased us to the room where we would be meeting the president of Mali. I was sitting next to the Canadian ambassador.

"It's dangerous to parade around the streets of Bamako like this," I whispered to him. "The mujahideen know exactly where we are, they could attack us."

I didn't feel safe, and I was anxious to leave Africa. The ambassador reassured me; Canada was seeing to our safety at all times. Luca seemed a little calmer than me, at least on the surface. I was glad he was with me.

The president soon entered and took his seat. Luca and I chatted with him for a while. When the discussion was over, he stood up to greet the audience and, before leaving the room, he humorously squirted hand sanitizer in each person's palm. We followed him outside, where he gave a speech to the journalists. I don't know what happened next, but someone pushed Luca and me next to the president. I was trying to look natural. I put my hands together in front of me, but I felt embarrassed. I glanced at Luca, who was watching a camera operator filming us. Luca seemed as awkward as I was.

When the president's speech was over, the woman from Global Affairs (let's call her Caroline) told us that we had to make one last stop before we could finally go to the Canadian embassy to rest, wash up, and eat. Mali wasn't done with us yet. We had to get back in the pickup truck, in the same crazy convoy that had brought us to the presidential palace.

After that, in yet another room, there were more questions to be answered. We were exhausted—the discussion had been going on for hours, and suddenly a man appeared, stammering a few words in French: that was how I met my Canadian security detail (let's call him Mr. Yung). What a memorable event—he was quite a character. I realized that he was Anglophone, and spoke only a little French, so I switched to English.

"Can I help you?"

He explained to me that he was trying to tell our interlocutors that their time was up, that we had to go back to the Canadian embassy. I was more than willing to wrap up the discussion. Everyone was understanding, and wished us good luck.

We followed Mr. Yung and Caroline back to their SUV—with bulletproof windows, we were told. We drove back through Bamako, at a normal speed this time, and incognito. Everyone was laughing and cracking jokes, and the driver whistled at the wheel. I was finally able to relax. I settled into my seat. We were in Canada's care now.

[44]

The Embassy

"WHAT WOULD YOU like to eat?" Caroline asked. She was sitting with us in the back seat.

"Fruit!" I shouted.

For fifteen months I had been dreaming of eating delicious, juicy, sweet, fresh fruit. I needed vitamins. Caroline laughed, and texted my request to her team.

"Luca loves mangoes," I added shyly.

She smiled again as she tapped in that detail. Shortly afterwards she received a reply from the embassy: our fruit would be waiting. Luca thanked her.

Mr. Yung, who was sitting in the front seat, turned to us.

"Welcome home."

We had arrived at the Canadian embassy.

"What do you want to do first?" Caroline asked us. "Shower? Eat? Rest?"

"I'd like to have a shower," I said. We could eat after. Luca nodded.

Someone opened the door and we got out of the car.

"I'll take you to your room," Caroline said.

It was a nice room on the second floor. There was even a welcome bag on the bed, with clothes, books, soaps, creams, perfumes, powder, blush, mascara. I think that was the first time in my life I was given makeup!

"*Cazzo!*" Luca exclaimed. "It's Christmas!"

We took advantage of the little break to rest and to make ourselves presentable before heading to our fruity feast.

"Are you ready, *principessa?*"

"Yes! I'm starving!"

On the way back down to the ground floor, we ran into Caroline.

"Follow me," she said.

In the dining room, several people were waiting patiently for our arrival around a large table heaped with food. I only had eyes for the array of exquisite fruit.

"We ransacked Bamako!" a young man said, placing a plate overflowing with perfectly cut mangoes on the table.

"Wow!" Luca exclaimed.

I didn't know it yet, but the stocky young man with the bald head was our doctor, Mr. Clean.

"There's also Thai and Indian food," Caroline said, sweeping her arm at the table.

I was excited to taste all the dishes. What a wonder!

We were introduced to the guests, men and women who had all come to Mali to solve the mystery of our disappearance, to find us. We were so moved.

During the meal, a man entered the room and walked toward Luca—a nervous Italian with long, flouncy hair. He explained to Luca that he could go to Germany if he wanted, of course, but that a plane could take him back to Italy that evening. Mr. Clean chimed in: the hospital in Germany was very good, and we would be well looked after. But Luca was listening to his fellow countryman, who was becoming a little more insistent.

"I'm going to go to Italy." Luca turned to me. "It's my country. I'm going to go home."

My heart tightened.

"Yes, I understand, Luca."

Everyone seemed disappointed, except the Italian emissary. The guests understood perfectly well why Luca wanted to return to his family, but this turn of events hit me hard. I wasn't prepared for him to leave me so soon. The Italian gave Luca his phone so he could call his family, and Luca got up from the table and left the room.

Seeing that Luca wasn't coming back right away, the doctor offered to examine me. He had been asked for a medical report as soon as possible, before I left Mali. I followed him to his office in a nearby room. After the examination, as the doctor and I were chatting, I saw Luca walking down the hall.

"I'm here!"

He turned back, and came into the exam room.

"I'm sorry, *principessa*," he said, crestfallen. "I have to go..."

"Already?"

"In ten minutes."

I was stunned. We immediately went back to our room. My stomach was in knots. I bit back my tears; I had to be strong. We talked for a few minutes, and then the Italian official knocked on the door.

"Goodbye, Luca. Give my love to your family."

I was stricken. Luca had left me again. My heart was breaking. I took a few moments to recover from my emotions, and then left the room. I had to call my family too.

A few minutes later, Caroline and I went back up to my room. She stopped at the door, dialed a number on her phone, and handed it to me. Before leaving, she turned back to me.

"Take your time. The plane leaves in an hour."

The phone rang—at home, on the other side of the world. The line buzzed in my ear. My heart was pounding!

"Hello..."

My mother's voice.

"*Maman!*"

"Oh, my God! My darling! How are you? Where are you?"

"I'm fine. I am at the embassy in Bamako. They're looking after me."

"I'm so glad to hear your voice!" I had never heard my mother sound so happy, so relieved. "Wait, I'm putting you on speaker, your sister's here."

"Hey sis!"

My sister's voice washed over me like a wave of love.

[45]

Germany

"OKAY... BYE! I love you! I'll see you in a week!"

It felt so good to finally talk to my mother and my sister, to know that they were both okay. A burden had been lifted from my shoulders. I felt lighter. Everything was fine. In all the long months I had been away from the world, nothing bad had happened to the people I loved. I wanted to call my father too, but Caroline turned up again.

"How are you?"

"Very well, thank you. I think everyone is relieved."

"I can imagine! Are you ready? It's time to go."

"Yes."

I would call my dad later.

On the way to the airport, my bodyguard, Mr. Yung, told me that we would be flying aboard a military cargo plane, a new model, the biggest one there was. It was the only plane available that night. Caroline had taken a pillow from my room and brought it with us, explaining that the plane wouldn't be very comfortable. I was about to find out exactly what she had meant.

At the airport, about ten people were in the VIP lounge with me. They all worked at the embassy, and had come to say goodbye and wish me a safe journey. Only three of them would be making the trip with me: the doctor, Mr. Clean; my bodyguard, Mr. Yung; and Caroline, from Global Affairs, who made sure I had everything I needed. They were so kind to me that I was flustered. But we laughed a lot too, and that made me feel good. The two men were real jokers, and Caroline was thoughtful and sincere. They touched my heart.

"So, what happened in the world in 2019?" I called out in the lounge.

One after the other, everyone told me about the key events of that year. We were chatting away, when I spotted a glorious orange in a fruit basket. Could I have it? Mr. Yung immediately dove for the orange.

"Let me peel it for you," he said, pulling a knife out of his pocket.

I was so taken aback by such an outpouring of kindness that my eyes welled up. I hid my tears. A few seconds later, he handed me the peeled fruit on a paper napkin.

"Your orange!"

What a gentleman! The three of them treated me like a princess until I returned to Canada. I smiled and thanked him, and decided to share the orange. Two or three men gladly took a piece. Then there was a knock on the door, and it was time to go. Before leaving, Mr. Yung winked at me and grabbed another orange for the road. I smiled at him again.

I followed my companions to... a monster! Was that a plane? For me? The aircraft, a Hercules, could carry tanks and fighter planes. A plane that can carry planes is a big plane indeed. Mr. Yung was amused by my astonishment.

"All for the four of us."

I didn't know what to say. We were so tiny compared to the behemoth! How could such a thing fly? I was fascinated. As we boarded, Caroline gave me the pillow from the embassy. I thanked her and sat down in one of the many folding seats against the steel of the hull. Two soldiers were acting as flight attendants. One of them came forward to explain safety instructions. The other gave us earplugs. I quickly understood why.

The monster started up and roared as it took to the sky, carrying us in its belly. It was deafening. Soon after, we were able to unbuckle our belts. My bodyguard got up immediately and walked to the middle of the plane, where there were several cardboard boxes. He motioned for me to come closer. We had to communicate by gestures because of the engine noise. What was he doing? Sitting on the floor, he opened the boxes one by one with enthusiasm. He pulled out a paper plate, and then a chicken skewer, pita bread, tabbouleh, hummus. There was a feast hidden in those boxes! He waved me over again. I sat down next to him, took the plate he handed me, and fixed myself a nice meal, like at a buffet. Caroline came to join us too. Mr. Clean was fast asleep in his chair, his chin against his chest. It was already late in the evening and we were all exhausted by the intensity of the events. My doctor had lost the battle against sleep before dinner.

Once we were done eating, I signaled to Mr. Yung that I wanted to sleep. One of the soldiers saw my gesture and hurriedly unfolded five or six seats that would serve as my bed, and laid a long piece of cardboard on top to fill the gaps. I thanked him and lay down with my pillow from the embassy and the blue blanket that the friendly French MINUSMA official had given us in Kidal. At last, I was in bed. The day had been endless, and I was bone-tired. The four hours of sleep I'd managed to get the previous night seemed far away. As for Mr. Yung, he lay on the floor in a sleeping bag.

I sighed and closed my eyes. Suddenly, I felt a presence next to me. It was Mr. Yung, who was offering me his sleeping bag. I thanked him with a wide smile and hardly hesitated before taking the treasure from his hands. A bed, a pillow, a blanket, a sleeping bag. What comfort! I was going to sleep like a log.

I closed my eyes... and opened them again.

There was movement in the Hercules. Mr. Clean signaled to me that we were preparing to land. What? I had only closed my eyes for ten minutes, or so it had seemed. But if we were nearing our destination in Germany, that meant we had been flying for nine hours. How could that be? I must have been completely wiped to have slept for so long, without moving a muscle, and despite such a racket.

As soon as the plane landed, we were able to take out our earplugs and finally talk to each other. Caroline asked me if I had slept well.

"Like a baby! I don't think I've ever slept so deeply in my life!"

The three of them laughed. I hadn't moved as much as an eyelash during the flight, they told me.

"And you? Did you sleep well?"

Their tired faces and red eyes spoke eloquently about the kind of night they'd spent.

"Not as well as you," Caroline replied with a smile.

When we climbed out of the plane, German nurses stopped us immediately: they had to take our temperature first and ask us questions. We weren't used to all the public health regulations surrounding the pandemic yet, because things were different in Africa. But at least we were able to get off the Hercules. I met the young man who would be looking after me during my stay in the hospital, a psychologist who specialized in post-traumatic stress disorder (I'll call him Jet Su). Mr. Clean and I followed him to the ambulance that would be taking us to the hospital, and Mr. Yung and Caroline headed to their hotel.

I was shown the wing of the hospital where I would be staying.

"It looks like there's no one there," I said, taken aback.

"That's because you're our only case right now," Jet Su said. "The whole wing is all yours."

I was shown to a room where I could find food and drink. For the first time in my life, I did a coffee dance! Jet Su laughed at how happy I was—I was literally overcome. I was then taken to my room, coffee in hand. Jet Su and Mr. Clean had to go and sort out a few things before I could officially be handed over to the Germans, and my psychologist suggested I go lie down. I agreed happily, I could use the rest. The medical examinations would only begin the next morning.

During the week I spent at the hospital, I had the chance to see my Canadian companions a few times. Jet Su organized two dinners so that we could just spend some time together. It felt good to relax with them. We got along well; we had fun and laughed all the time. Jet Su was hilarious, too.

The day I finally received my new contact lenses, I was so excited that I couldn't sit still. Finally, I would be able to see what was going on around me, I would be able to make out the expressions and emotions of the people around me. I popped them in the second I got them.

Standing in front of the bathroom mirror, I stopped to consider the reflection of this girl who didn't expect to see me so clearly. So this was the face of the little human slowly returning to life. I touched my face, the new wrinkles that had appeared during the long struggle. Then I went to meet up with the other humans who were busy in the hospital. It was a pleasure to watch them work. I wasn't very well going to stay shuttered meekly in my room.

Just then, Jet Su arrived.

"Good morning, Mr. Su. You look different today," I said as we greeted each other in the hallway outside my room.

"Did you get your contact lenses?"

I nodded, smiling broadly.

"So now you can see that I'm Italian!" he joked.

Actually, his father was Italian and his mother was Korean, but he looked Asian, hence the joke.

He handed me a box, explaining that it contained letters from family and friends, as well as photos of my niece and nephew, and paintings they'd made me. I felt a flood of emotion come over me, and had to turn away to hide my tears. What a surprise, what a joy! Jet Su was looking at me kindly; he'd seen the tears. I wiped them away with the back of my hand, then took the box and ran to my bed to make myself comfortable. Jet Su came and sat on the edge of the mattress, and asked me how I was doing.

"Do you feel like you're able to look through what's in there on your own, or would you prefer me to stay close by?"

"I'd rather be alone," I replied, beaming.

Jet Su nodded, waved, and walked away, leaving me alone with all those messages of love. I took the lid off and dipped my hand in the box, leaving it up to chance to determine what I would read first.

The first letter was from my beloved grandmother! I drank in her words of tenderness and hope.

"I'm waiting for you with open arms. I want to hold you against my heart. Come back to us glowing! I love you, my free spirit."

I was touched to the core of my being. I read every single letter, wetting them with my tears.

"Every night I look up at the sky and think that maybe we're looking at the same stars."

"Welcome home, to your childhood land, even though I know that your real home is in your heart, no matter where you are!"

I was picking through the messages at random, so I didn't read them in chronological order. Some had been written recently, after our escape had been announced, while others were from January 2019, and others still from December, just after we had disappeared.

"We think about you all the time here. We wonder what you are doing, how you are doing, if you are being treated well, and if you can talk to anyone. I imagine you with your toes in the sand, living a life rooted in the wilderness of the African desert, surviving. I know in my heart that if anyone can get through it, you can! Do you remember those stories about how you'd show *Maman* how you could lift walls, or cars? I think back to that when I want to remember the strength that lies within you."

"I wish I could write to you every day, endlessly. I think I do a bit in my head, and I try to remember all the beautiful moments so we can tell you about them one day! Hopefully I'll be able to write to you again, and hopefully we won't have to write to each other anymore, because you'll finally be back home!"

"May your natural radiance protect you from evil, hunger, and thirst."

"My beautiful friend, my beautiful love, I am with you every moment, every breath, every heartbeat. I love you like the light of the moon, the sun, and the stars together. All my thoughts of love and light are with you."

"We thought about you every day. Every morning we got up and thought *Is today the day?* You're free at last! We can't wait to give you a hug."

I paused, to try to stop crying. I reached for the two paintings at the bottom of this treasure chest, by one of my nieces and one of my nephews. What a thing it must have been for my sister to explain to her children what had happened to me. They had written me messages, too. I unfolded the paper with their names on it, intrigued.

"Welcome home *matante* Edith, I can't wait to see you again!" That was Félix, who was thirteen.

"Hello Edith, I hope you are feeling well now that we have found you, I can't wait to see you again! I love you very much," Gabriel, twelve years old, had written.

"Dear Edith, I love you very much, I have really looked forward to the time when we would meet again, I can't wait to see you. See you soon!" My niece Maïka was nine years old.

"Dear Edith, we are happy to see you again, we all love you lots. We were worried about you, we're so glad to get to see you again!" Ysée was seven.

After a fifteen-month nightmare, these loving words were a breath of life. The pendulum was swinging back, a gift.

[46]

Canada

BEFORE I LEFT Germany, Jet Su told me that sometimes PTSD victims are so upset when they arrive that they can't even step into the hospital. Jet Su adapts to the condition of each person, treating them individually.

"You'll be fine," he said, hugging me and reminding me that I was resilient, I was brave. "Call me anytime," he added.

I was still shaken from my fifteen months of captivity, but I felt pretty good, considering. And I was ready to go home. Back to real life! Luca and I were lucky that we'd been able to keep our cool during such an extreme experience. I truly believe that the fact that we had triumphed over our enemies together had a big impact on how we felt now—it helped heal the wounds.

I thanked my psychologist for his kind words, his support and sensitivity, and then I boarded the small plane that was waiting. I was still accompanied by my lovely trio, as well as two women I had met at the hospital. One worked for the Royal Canadian Mounted Police, and the other was a colleague of Mr. Clean's, who until then had stayed in the background, like many others. I was never introduced to most of the people working behind the scenes. I think it was at the request of Jet Su, who wanted to keep contact to a minimum while I was being rehabilitated. Apart from Jet Su,

I had met with an ophthalmologist, a dentist, a physiotherapist, a nutritionist, several doctors, and some support staff at the hospital. And in my spare time, between medical examinations, counter-terrorism specialists had come to interview me. Everyone else had held back. Jet Su wanted me to get some fresh air before I went home; this was an in-between time, a time to get my strength back before I went on my way. He was protective, and tried to pave the way for recovery. Before I got on the plane, I turned to him to wave goodbye, and he responded in kind, patiently waiting to watch his patient take to the skies.

They explained that, due to the aircraft's low fuel capacity, we would be making two stops, first on a small Portuguese island in the Azores, and then in Nova Scotia. Clearly, the cute, tiny plane was the logical continuation of the trip on the gargantuan freighter. The story of my life—from one extreme to the other. There were five seats and a bench in the cabin. My doctor pointed to the long, comfortable bench seat with cushions and blankets piled on top.

"For you," he said.

"Wow! Thank you! You guys are great. This is even better than a VIP flight."

I made myself a cozy little bed for the journey. I had accumulated a lot of fatigue over the past year and a half, never getting much sleep at night among the fanatical, armed mujahideen, and now I was making the most of the comfort I was offered. I'm sure they could see stars shining in my eyes. My companions were clearly gratified to see me smiling so much too.

Whoops; I'd forgotten to buckle up for takeoff. I straightened up and fastened my seatbelt. The so-called flight attendant introduced himself before we left, and I knew right away that we would be well looked after. He was attentive, offering me pistachios and brownies, but I wasn't hungry. It was funny to see soldiers playing the role of flight attendants—they were the opposite of the stereotypical style.

As soon as I could, I crawled under the covers to rest. Shortly afterwards, the flight attendant offered me food—a most tempting menu, nothing short of a three-course meal. For the main course I had salmon, and after eating I closed my eyes. When I opened them, I found a bag of pistachios on the table in front of me. I smiled. The others hadn't had any, and I told them they could have mine. Later, after I had dozed off again, I discovered a brownie on the small table. I was delighted.

At one point, after several hours, the pilot himself came to see me.

"Would you like to come up to the cockpit? We'll be landing in the Azores in a few minutes."

"Okay!"

What a thrill! As he sat back into his seat, the pilot introduced me to the copilot, who would be handling the landing. During the descent, the pilot chatted away about the various maneuvers, even throwing in a few jokes. But at a certain altitude, they had to concentrate, and he fell silent. I was enjoying the show. The island looked so lush and green from the sky, as the ocean calmly nuzzled it with its ripples. Down on the ground, a tiny little man was waving at us, showing us where to land. We touched down gently. The copilot had landed without a hitch. I thanked the two men for allowing me to share such a special moment with them, and, along with the other five passengers, I got out of the plane to stretch my legs while we refueled.

I hadn't been expecting it to be so cold and windy, though we were in the middle of the North Atlantic, after all. My bodyguard, noticing that I wasn't dressed properly, gave me his coat. Truly, what a gentleman! I had spent fifteen months feeling like a worthless commodity, convinced that Canada would never pay ransom. And now, since the previous week, I was being treated like a jewel. It goes to show that you never know what to expect: life always has surprises in store. Sometimes it can be scary, it can hurt, but

I decided to take it as it came, trials and all, and to do whatever I could to come out on top.

I looked at Mr. Yung in his light short-sleeved shirt; he had goosebumps.

"Take your coat, you're cold!"

"I am never cold!" he lied.

The pilot was waving at us; we were ready to take off again.

During the second part of the trip, we had a meal worthy of a five-star restaurant. The flight attendant, it turned out, was also the chef. How did he manage to do all that without a kitchen on board? It was a mystery, but a tasty one.

The flight was long, and near the end the doctor was getting antsy. He got up and did some yoga in the aisle. I suggested he do a headstand. To my amazement, this massive, muscular man placed his bald head on the floor and began to raise his legs. Mr. Yung leapt up behind him as if to catch him, assuming he might have a hard time holding the position in a moving plane. He wanted to make sure he didn't punch a hole in the floor of the plane if he fell backward. I burst out laughing. Those two were such comedians. Mr. Clean obviously wasn't going do anything reckless; he just wanted to make me laugh.

After refueling in Nova Scotia, we headed for Montreal, the last stop on our long journey, though the pilot later informed us that strong winds over Montreal meant that we would have to land in Ottawa. It complicated things a little, but within an hour, everything was settled: a car would take me to Sherbrooke, to my mother's house.

Caroline had told me that our arrival would be calm, that there would be no journalists there when we landed. No one wanted to relive the scene in Bamako, and that made me feel better. I have nothing against journalists, but I've never liked being the center of attention.

It was well into the night by the time I got into the car and we left Ottawa. I took the phone numbers of my three wonderful companions with me. They made me promise to call them if I was back in Ottawa. I was sad to leave. I had grown fond of them, and they had been such a help to me since we'd met.

The three-hour drive went by quickly; once again, fatigue got the best of me. When I opened my eyes again, I recognized the city right away. We were in Sherbrooke! We would be getting to my mother's house soon. My heart was pounding.

The car turned into the driveway. All the lights in the house were on. I got out of the car and climbed the front steps.

"*Maman*! I'm here!" I shouted from the doorway.

My mother ran to me.

"Oh! Darling! My darling! I was so worried, if you only knew. I'm so happy to be able to hold you, to see you."

She hugged me tight, so tight.

Life

Among the mountains she painted
He walked, and here was everything—
Like snow on the pines—he'd ever wanted.
She exhaled clouds and of rain they sang.

He moved with life inspired, divine,
Holding a hand in the storm.
She swept leaves into the spiraling
Wind, his gaze on her like a balm.

He listened each time to what she could see
And she found herself in a painting.
She changed the colors with whim and glee
To find the ones that pleased him.

They laughed and laughed and drank too much wine,
Free from what madness was lurking.
She offered him fruit, ripe and so fine,
And built hives for pleasure and sweetness.

They journeyed through winter in the Canadian north.
They ran through fields with bees in the grass.
She knew one day they would have to part
And took him in her arms for one last kiss.

With Barbarossa

 The women's camp

 Solitary captivity

 Suleiman and Asiya

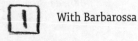 Luca's estimate of our position when he drew the placement of the camp in the sand. In reality, we were in Zone 4.

 Capture

 Road trip

 Path in captivity

 Niger River

 Adrar des Ifoghas (rock desert)

W Park

SENEGAL

GUINEA

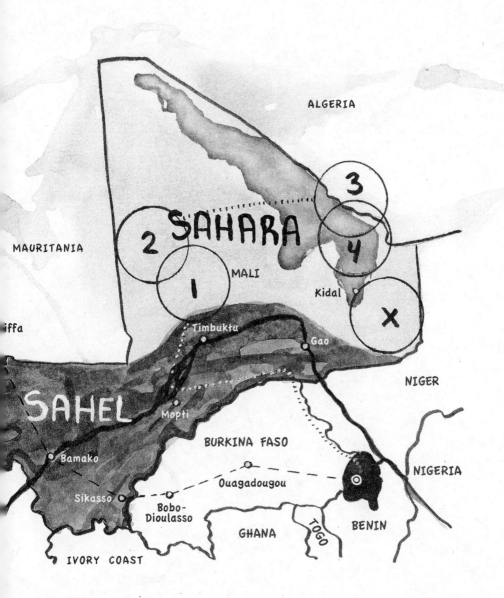

A Letter to Life

IT IS SEPTEMBER 14, 2020, in Canada, the year 1442 in Islamic countries.

We think the Earth is 4.54 billion years old, but I believe the universe is beyond the limit of our mathematics.

I am sitting on a rock on the banks of the Athabasca River near Jasper, a small town in western Alberta, a province of Canada. Canada is a country in North America, a continent on Earth. We have delineated the territories, named them.

Territorial and religious divisions have always puzzled me.

Diversity is beautiful and essential, so why does it so often carry the stench of blood and war? As though we weren't all born on the same earth, as though we weren't made of the same dust.

Whoever is convinced that theirs is the lone truth is potentially dangerous. That much was made clear to me many times during my captivity.

Some people say that you, Life, can be cruel. Are they right?

I ask the question, and I await your answer.

You too are writing a letter to me in your own way. You are not human, so your letter wouldn't be made of words, but rather images, smells, sensations. Your answer is here, before me. Today you have misted the mountains, up there, at the very top. Your message is cold, and the wind delivers it forcefully. I have heard your voice—the cry of a raven. You whisper to me in the river that surges to my left. Today, your answer does not lie in the sun, which is stuck behind the clouds.

I took off my shoes to lay my bare feet against you, but your pebbles are cold. The smell of fir followed me all through the forest. I wonder how many fir trees there can be around me. I can't count them, so many are hidden by fog. You don't want to tell me the answer; you like to keep your secrets.

Do you remember when I was a captive in the desert? My eyesight was blurred, and I had lost the beauty of your images. Was that to make me appreciate them all the more once my sight was restored? If so, it worked. When I was separated from Luca in the desert, did you want me to learn to love even more dearly the wealth and weight of everything he brought me? If so, well, it worked. Did I lose my freedom so that I could value every moment once I had it back? When I had no food or water, was it to learn to savor and honor what grows on you, what you offer us as a gift? It worked.

I look at the river and my face ripples on your waters. I am looking at my reflections.

Maybe I should appreciate these teachings because I've grown, and because I'm grateful for all that you offer me. We are on earth to evolve and to learn, right? Does that mean I would choose the same path again, knowing how it ends? No, never. I suffered a lot over there. I often thought I would lose my life, and, when I was completely isolated, I feared I would lose my mind.

But how could I find you rude or unforgiving? How could I now be afraid? It was the men who held me, not you: you offer us so much beauty and possibility, yet we don't always make good use of it.

Thank you for helping us during our escape on March 13, 2020. You blurred our tracks with the wind and sent us a guardian angel, a man who risked his life to help bring us back to freedom.

Men can be cruel, but they can also be good.

I will cherish these hard-earned lessons. I have learned not to take anything for granted. We become aware of what we have once we have lost it; only then do we see that the richness of life is in the simplest things.

Yours,
A HUMAN

A Letter From Luca

Tuesday, October 13, 2020

We've been home for a few months now, and I'm only just beginning to realize that we are actually free. I wake up in the morning and I can wander as I want. I take a deep breath and the air is fine. I drink a glass of wine and my teeth are stained with red. There are no culprits, no winners or losers. We managed to recover the life that the Kalashnikovs took from us, before it was too late. I keep thinking about those who are still in captivity, there or elsewhere in the world. We can now attest that losing your freedom is hard. Thankfully, for us, it's over.

I returned to Italy in the springtime, as flowers spattered the meadows all the way to the horizon. I saw the summer pass, heard waves breaking on the sand—not so different, perhaps, from the desert sand, but everything seems more peaceful with the sea tumbling by, the repeated lull of the waves. The seasons passed, and autumn came with the joy of the harvest. As a family we picked our grapes and made our wine, and my fingers are crossed that it will be a good year. Now winter is here, and I am in the mountains. The snow is beginning to cover the peaks. Everything is so perfect that sometimes my heart weeps with happiness. I don't remember

whether I was so aware of every little breath before this experience: the past is already beginning to be lost in the mist.

Edith used to sing a song that's still going through my head—
"*Que sera, sera.*" What will be, will be.

Thanks be to life!

LUCA TACCHETTO

Al-Qaeda in the Heart of West Africa

By DAVID MORIN *and* FRANÇOIS AUDET

I T'S NOT EASY to make sense of armed jihad and the dynamics of terrorism in Africa. They involve multiple players, and various motives and strategies. Throughout her book, Edith uses several terms and names that may not be familiar to some readers: the Group for the Support of Islam and Muslims (JNIM); jihad, jihadists, mujahideen; Iyad Ag Ghaly, Amadou Koufa. She also references the Fula people, the Tuareg, and Arabs. Who are these individuals and groups? What exactly do they want? And, most importantly, why did they take Edith and Luca?

During the fifteen months of Edith's captivity, my colleague François Audet and I were called upon to comment on the case in the media because of our respective fields of expertise. We also had the privilege of playing an advisory role with Edith's family, which quickly became a friendship as far as I was concerned, since I was in constant contact with the family. It was both as consultants and as family friends that we were asked to write a brief word—I insisted on brevity!—to clarify certain notions for readers interested in a deeper understanding of Edith's captivating story.

JIHADISM IN WEST AFRICA

Edith was abducted in Burkina Faso, then taken to Mali, where she was held captive. For several years, West Africa has been plagued by growing insecurity, notably due to the presence of non-state armed groups and bandits (often called "road cutters"), but also due to the rise of jihadist terrorist groups that have formed since the end of the Algerian Civil War and the conflicts in Libya, Syria, and Iraq. These groups are referred to as "jihadists" because their fighters, called mujahideen, advocate armed jihad, an Islamist religious and political ideology that uses violence to establish an Islamic state and Islamic, or sharia, law. In the absence of effective state governance, security, social equity, and economic opportunity, these groups are recruiting or forcibly conscripting large numbers of young people from various communities in the region.

Jihadist groups are numerous and vary greatly in size. They evolve rapidly, forming and dissolving, and changing their names and affiliations. They may have different approaches depending on their particular demands, sources of income, areas of operation, ethnicity or identity, and local roots. They take advantage of local sociopolitical and cultural situations to further their interests and carry out their actions, and they may forge temporary or longer-term alliances with other jihadist groups, other armed groups, or different local communities. Edith and Luca were captured by members of Ansarul Islam and transferred to the JNIM.

At times, jihadist groups fight among themselves—for instance, some of the JNIM-allied groups affiliated with Al-Qaeda have had violent clashes with the Daesh-affiliated Islamic State in the Greater Sahara.

GROUP FOR THE SUPPORT OF ISLAM AND MUSLIMS

Under the leadership of the Malian Tuareg commander Iyad Ag Ghaly, the JNIM was formed in 2017 out of the consolidation of several organizations. Among the best known, Al-Qaeda in the

Islamic Maghreb (AQIM) has made kidnapping a major source of revenue, amassing nearly $125 million, according to a *New York Times* investigation published in 2014. It was AQIM that took Canadian diplomats Robert Fowler and Louis Guay hostage in 2008 in the region. Another JNIM-affiliated group is the Macina Liberation Front, led by the Fula leader and emir Amadou Koufa. Several fighters who were guarding Edith claimed that he was their leader.

Not all of these individuals and groups were originally proponents of armed jihad. Before becoming a jihadist, Iyad Ag Ghaly was an important figure in the Tuareg uprisings in the 1990s in Mali, rebellions that reflected the discontent of a segment of the nomadic populations in the country's north who never really recognized themselves in integration attempts and who have long made political demands for autonomy and independence. Amadou Koufa was first a preacher from the Fula community, pastoralists established throughout West Africa, who denounced the social hierarchies in place and the lack of options for African youth. The Fula were known political stakeholders in the region, with a deep history, who maintained links with various political, military, religious, and community authorities in the country. Nonetheless, whether through opportunism or conviction, they embraced jihadism, and are engaged in varying degrees of confrontation with local governments and armed forces. They also face the United Nations Multidimensional Integrated Stabilization Mission in Mali (MINUSMA) and foreign powers, notably France and its Barkhane military operation, whose drones, feared by the jihadists, flock over the desert.

MOTIVES FOR TAKING HOSTAGES

The reasons behind hostage-taking are numerous and often interconnected. It is important to note that in West Africa, as elsewhere, the overwhelming majority of hostages are local victims. While

Western nationals are more seldom captured, their value to these jihadist groups is significant: hostages can be used as a source of income if their country of origin, or another agency or individual, agrees to pay a ransom for their release. This practice is contrary to international conventions on the financing of terrorism, and governments officially reject ransoming, though the practice remains common. Hostages may also be used as bargaining chips, for instance for the release of jihadist prisoners, or in exchange for other concessions. Finally, hostage-taking can be a means of blackmail or propaganda for political demands, especially when hostages are threatened or executed. In other words, hostages are precious assets for these groups, who devote considerable human resources to holding them captive. It is understandable, then, that captivity and negotiations sometimes last for months or even years.

For the hostages, there are fewer options: Release without compensation, which is not usual for Westerners. Release following negotiations, as was the case with Fowler and Guay in 2008. Extraction in a military or police operation, which can go wrong. Successful escape, which is rare. Or death, as was sadly the case of Kirk Woodman, a Canadian geologist who was kidnapped and killed in Burkina Faso a few days after Edith and Luca's abduction. As Edith's 450-day-long ordeal suggests, the passage of time rarely works in hostages' favor. The conditions in which they are detained are harsh, and their health deteriorates as the weeks go by; their lives often hang by a thread.

At this point, you already know more than Edith, her family, and we did at the time of her abduction. Edith's beautiful story is full of solitude and silence—the silence of the men who held her captive, but also the silence that generally surrounds a kidnapping of this kind. It is easy, then, to imagine what an ordeal a situation like this is for a hostage's family and relatives, who are often overlooked. On our side, supporting the family in developing a strategy, with the considerable involvement of our networks in Canada and internationally, was an extraordinary professional and human experience, which happily culminated in meeting Edith—free. The rest of this remarkable story is hers to tell.

DAVID MORIN
Professor at the School of Applied Politics of the Université de Sherbrooke and co-chairholder of the UNESCO Chair in the Prevention of Radicalization and Violent Extremism (UNESCO-PREV)

FRANÇOIS AUDET
Associate Professor at the School of Management Sciences of the Université du Québec à Montréal and Director of the Canadian Research Institute on Humanitarian Crises and Aid (OCCAH)

Acknowledgments

I N STRUGGLING TO find the right words to convey the extent of my gratitude, I find instead only commonplace expressions that fall short: *I can't thank you enough*, or *my undying thanks for your generosity, your time, your talent, and, above all, your love.*

Thanks to my favorite sister, Mélanie Bergeron Blais, for being my fine-toothed comb. The subtle details that you worked so hard—albeit lovingly!—to get me to write added such life and color to the story. Thank you for your support and dedication. You were with me throughout this project on every level. And these acknowledgments wouldn't be complete without noting that, whatever you might think, you really are the businesswoman in the family.

Thank you to my dear friend, poet Annick Boivin, who so graciously accompanied me throughout my writing journey. Your subtle touch made the book that much better.

Thank you to my editor, Ann Châteauvert, for your sensitivity, your gentleness, and your commitment. I'm so glad that our paths crossed on this adventure.

Thank you to the teams at Éditions de l'Homme and Greystone Books for your enthusiasm, kindness, and passion.

Thank you to Luca Tacchetto for supporting and accompanying me through our ordeal: love and gratitude will always be etched on my heart.

Thank you to my mother, Jocelyne Bergeron, for being my first reader. Thank you for your encouragement and for sharing the emotions that stirred within you. Thank you for being my biggest fan.

Thank you to David Desmarais, my best friend, for all the love, friendship, and magic you lavish on me.

Thank you to my father, André Blais, to my grandmothers, Madeleine Bergeron and Paula Lemire, to my stepmother, Marie-Hélène Granger, and to my friends, aunts, uncles, and cousins for your love, joy, and comfort.

Thank you to all those who did everything they could to bring me home safe and sound.

Finally, I would like to thank those who thought of us and carried us in their hearts during our captivity, and again when we came home. I know that you went a long time without any news, and that I was rather private when I arrived. Thank you for your patience and respect.

By way of thanks, I am ready, at last, to share my story.

TRANSLATOR'S ACKNOWLEDGMENTS
Thanks to Capt. Sébastien Côté for consulting on military aircraft, Dr. Jeffrey Heath for his expertise in Tamasheq, and Elisabeth Jaquette for revising the Arabic.